AF539785

India and Central Asia

A Shared Past

By the same author

1. Illegal Migration from Bangladesh
2. India and Central Asia: Classical to Contemporary Periods
3. Naga Identity
4. Problems of Ethnicity in the North-East India
5. Small States Syndrome in India
6. Rashtriya Samasyaen: Chinta avem Chintan (Hindi)

About the Author

Dr. B.B. Kumar, (b.1941), M.Sc. (Chemistry), M.Sc. (Anthropology), M.A. (Hindi), Ph.D. (Anthro.), former Principal, Sao Change Government College, Tuensang (Nagaland), and Science College, Kohima, was Member, Executive Council, Academic Council, University Court, College Development Council, Examination Committee, School Board of Physical Sciences and other numerous committees of the North-Eastern Hill University, Shillong (India). He was Chairman, Hindi Board of Studies, and Member, Board of Studies, of 'Science for Rural Development', Gandhigram Rural University, Tamil Nadu. He remained associated with a large number of NGOs as President, Vice President, Secretary and Member. He was founder Secretary of Nagaland Bhasha Parishad and Thinkers Forum, Nagaland and Governing Body Member of the Nagaland Peace Centre, the organization founded by Jai Prakash Narayan. He was Founder-Secretary, Astha Bharati, New Delhi, and Founder-Member, Governing Body of India Central Asia Foundation, New Delhi.

Dr. Kumar has written/edited/co-authored 136 books and more than 100 papers. Presently, he is editing Quarterly Journals, *Dialogue* (English) and *Chintan-Srijan* (Hindi), both published from Delhi, and *Quest*, the journal of the Vivekanand Kendra Institute of Culture, Guwahati. Some of his English language publications are *India; Caste, Culture and Traditions; A Macro Perception of the Tribal Societies of India; Small States Syndrome in India; Naga Identity; Tension and Conflict in North-East India; Illegal Migration from Bangladesh (Ed.), Modernization in Naga Society (Ed.); Ethnic Movements in North-East India;* and *India and Central Asia: Classical to Contemporary Period (Co-edited).*

India and Central Asia

A Shared Past

B.B. Kumar

CONCEPT PUBLISHING COMPANY PVT. LTD.
NEW DELHI-110059

ISBN-13: 978-93-5125-125-5

First Published 2015

Published and Printed by

Concept Publishing Company Pvt. Ltd.
A/15-16, Commercial Block, Mohan Garden
New Delhi-110059 (India)
T: 25351460, 25351794, *F*: 091-11-25357109
E: publishing@conceptpub.com, W: www.conceptpub.com
Editorial Office: H-13, Bali Nagar, New Delhi-110 015, India.

Cataloging in Publication Data--Courtesy: D.K. Agencies (P) Ltd. <docinfo@dkagencies.com>

Kumāra, Braja Bihārī, 1941- author.
India and Central Asia : a shared past / B.B. Kumar.
pages cm
Includes bibliographical references and index.
ISBN 9789351251255

1. India--Relations--Asia, Central. 2. Asia, Central--Relations--India. I. Title.

DDC 327.54058 23

Foreword

B.B. Kumar's survey of the cultural interflow between India and multi-ethnic, multi-linguistic and polycentric kingdoms of Central Asia reminds me of the Larkana Gazette on Mohenjodaro written in 1926 by officials of the British Raj. "The beauty of the dilapidated buildings and of articles discovered speaks volumes for ancient India and proves the truth of the historical statement, that in ancient times India was a great and powerful country and was not helpless as she is now. In view of this evidence of India's ancient greatness, Britain should treat her, if not as a superior, at least as an equal and respect her and set her free immediately." The translations of travel accounts of Chinese pilgrims by French scholars, the discovery of Sanskrit manuscripts in Japan by Prof. Max Muller, the opening up of chandis and lontars in Indonesia by Dutch masterminds, the deciphering of Sanskrit inscriptions from Cambodia and Champa (now the coastline of Vietnam) by savants in their studies in Paris were an 'eye-gift' to a renascent India waking up to her new tryst with freedom after centuries of oblivion. Likewise, the excavations in Central Asia conducted by British, French, German, Russian and Japanese expeditions were a celebration of the monumental cultural efflorescence during the first millennium in the arts, literature, philosophy and polity of the "thirty-six kingdoms" (to use a Chinese enumeration) in the vast sands of the Tarim basin and its surrounding environs. The austere landscape, the idyllic serenity of the murals and sculptures of the caves in the glory of their colours, in spite of vandalism and natural decay, were the subtle flavour of Dharma portraying the flowering of the mind. Acaryas and transnational merchants, intrepid young adventurers seeking greener pastures and the "global vision" of Ashoka became instrumental in converting tribal chieftains into larger formations of kingdoms. The peoples of Central Asia got their scripts from India, which were a must for communication in large states being established on the basis of common linguistic legacy of tribes.

Sanskrit culture reached Central Asia in the *dhammavijaya* of Ashoka, who gave up war at Kalinga and silenced the drums of war into drums of sharing values. *Bherighoṣa* became *Dhammaghoṣa.* Chinese and Tibetan accounts associate the foundation of the State of Khotan to the son and ministers of Ashoka. He initiated the influence of Sanskrit and the setting up of states on what was to become the Silk Route or rather the *Sutra* Route. Khotan became a major centre of Mahayana and has yielded the earliest version of the *Dharmapada* in the Prakrit of Gandhara in Kharosthi script. A version of the *Asokavadana,* extant only in Chinese translation, mentions Kucha as "one of the parts of his great empire which Ashoka proposed to give to his son Kunala". Ashoka relics, Ashoka-temples and Ashokastupas are being found in China to this day. The Tonyukuk epitaph mentions a king of the Sogdians named Asoqa. The Russian chronicles name the Prince of the Voguls in Northern Siberia as Asyka. Vogul folk-songs recall the glories of Osx or Ashoka.

Sanskrit literature is replete with references to the Turks as Tura, Turakvāḥ (plural), Turuṣka, to the Sogdians as *Śūlikāh,* to Tashkent as Dāksikantha or Kaṅka : *kaṅka* and *tash* both mean 'stone' and hence they are also known as *aśmaka.* The *Kalpanā-maṇḍitikā* of Kumaralata mentions that a painter from Puskalavati visited Aśmaka (=Tashkent) to decorate a monastery. Sanskrit became the cultural identity of the peoples of Central Asia and it gave a shared identity to Iranian Khotanese and Sogdians, European Tocharians, Altaic Huns, Turks and Uigurs, Yueh-chis and various other ethnicities. While local languages were the media of conversation and administration written in Indian scripts, Sanskrit was the idiom of intellectuals.

Kumarajiva studied Buddhism in Kashmir, but the Vedas with their six auxiliary sciences (*Sadāṅga*) in Kashgar. Several recensions of the *Yajurveda* were prevalent in Svetadvipa or Kucha, as discovered in a manuscript of *śākhā-vṛkṣa* by my father Prof. Raghuvira.

Hundreds of great minds of India have trod the inhospitable terrains of Central Asia for centuries sans end. Their very names are lost in the amnesia of time. Dr. B.B. Kumar closes his moving narrative of India's feel in the ruins of the Taklamakan desert by a sketch of Kumarajiva's contributions to East Asian cultures.

The magnetic pulse-beats of Kumarajiva's renderings became murals, reliefs and sculptures that have moved the people and are still a journey of Dharma. The lucidity of his expression has been the radiance, the silent spell, the magnetic joyfulness of the Dharma life of East Asia. Today his translation of the Lotus Sutra is the sound, grace and rapture of East Asian spirituality of values, for instance in the lovely blue of the Soka Gakkai International steeped in the strivings of President Daisaku Ikeda. The Six Principles of Painting of Hsieh Ho go back to Kumarajiva's translation of the *Satya-siddhi-sastra.* These principles have been, and still are, the bedrock of East Asian aesthetics. Kumarjiva was the trifluence of the three major alphabetic cultures of his time : Indian (Sanskrit as the classical language of his learning), Kuchean (his mother-tongue), and Chinese (medium of his immortal writings).

Dr. B.B. Kumar celebrates the tranquillity of thought and transcendence in silent stones and manuscripts torn into fragments in the fury of fundamentalist anger. His is an effort to work out a paradigm of a culture from stray references in Sanskrit and Chinese and from the idyllic serenity of the murals in the caves. It is a visual slip into the obscure flavours of Dharma lying in ancient ruins. This book incarnates the spirit of the Hsiao-yao Garden, which was placed at the disposal of Kumarajiva by Emperor Yao Hsing where a thousand monks sat in daily sessions to transcreate Sutras. Hsiao-yao means pleasant abstraction to cross the bounds of the physical universe to a blissful infinite beyond. Likewise, the dedication of a thousand scholars of a century have become the light of Dharma in the words of Dr. Kumar. Indian and Central Asian gurus in their angelic gaze from heaven admire this magnificent recount of the 'leaf books' (palm leaf manuscripts) and clouds of sandal wood incense of *dharmamegha samadhi* in the grottos. Dr. Kumar tries to radiate the magnificent hearts and hard journeying of Indic culture to bring mind's luminosity to the Sogdians, Khotanese, Tokharians, Hunas, Yueh-chihs and many other peoples. This book invites Young India to feel the depth within in the cosmic waters of Dharma.

Lokesh Chandra

Introduction

Central Asia is situated at the crossroads of the Great Silk Route and one of the most ancient world civilizations emerged in this region. Prosperous empires and kingdoms there have left a bright impact on the development of world culture. Ibn Ali Sinnah, Abu Rehon Beruni, Ahmad Al-Ferghani, Imam Al-Bukhari and several others have contributed to world culture.

Central Asia is blessed with an abundance of natural resources. With energy security now at the centre of the stage, Central Asia is drawing international attention. Major Powers and multinational companies need access to these resources and have concerns about the maintenance of favourable conditions for trade and commerce. For India, the developments in Central Asia would continue to be important as the region is part of its extended neighbourhood.

While discussing India's relations with Central Asia, it is rather difficult to separate the past from the present. The past feeds and enriches the present and provides the ambience for the warm relations that exist between us. Al-Beruni travelled from Khiva to India in 11th century and wrote *Kitab-Takkik Al-Hind.* This is one of the most authoritative books on Indian society and culture. According to an estimate, over three hundred manuscripts on the history and literature of Central Asia are available in Indian libraries, especially in Khudabakhsh library in Patna, Bihar State and Reza Library in Rampur, Uttar Pradesh.

In the middle of twentieth century the works of Khwaja Ahmad Abbas, Prem Chand, Rabindranath Tagore, Ali Sardar Jafree, Sajjad Zaheer and Amrita Preetam were translated into local languages and enjoyed popularity among readers. Poems of Mirza Abdul Qadir Bedil are taught at schools in Central Asia. These are the stances of very rich and deep cultural roots between Indians and people from Central Asia.

In the field of cultural cooperation between India and the Central Asia, I will find it extremely difficult to summarize the state of our relations. The setting up of the Indian Cultural Centres in Tashkent, Dushanbe and Almaty is a fitting testimony to this reality.

This book recapitulates the threads of old linkages with Central Asia. It contains a detailed examination of cultural, historical and social aspects of life in Central Asia.

I commend Dr. B. B. Kumar for his scholarship.

I hope that this book would contribute towards a greater and enlightened appreciation of India's relations with Central Asia espeically in historical and cultural arena.

Padma Bhushan K. Santhanam,
President,
India- Central Asia Foundation
03 January 2015, New Delhi

Preface

Indian links with the Central Asia–the Tarim basin, and the neighbouring Oxus region and the Badakshan, since antiquity, have been deep and multi-faceted. In reality, the two regions have been part of the same cultural and religious commonwealth; as the study reveals, we have been the cultural and the religious cousins. Noted British historian Toynbee, at least takes our linkages up to 1700 years before the Christ. The American scholar, Ellsworth Huntington (The Pulse of Asia), points towards our ethnic linkages. My endeavour to study and understand Central Asia has helped me in many ways; it has helped in the reduction of my conceptual haziness about India and its culture, and to some extent, in the reduction of my own cultural illiteracy. In reality, the understanding of India's cultural neighbourhood is essential for its own self-portrayal.

So far Central Asia is concerned; we had scholars, such as Professor Raghu Vira, Dr. B.N. Puri, Dr. P.C. Bagchi and Rahul Sankrityayan, who had done commendable work in promoting our understanding of the region, Professor Lokesh Chandra, soil of Professor Raghu Vira has in depth understanding of the same. But sometimes, our eminent scholars tend to generalize and confuse. Amartya Sen, for example, in his essay 'China and India' (*The Argumentative Indian's 2006*), points out "If China was enriching the material world two thousand years ago, India was busy, it appears, exporting Buddhism to China." Amartya Sen should have known that India, two thousand years ago, was not only a soft 'power', but a 'hard power', stronger than China. It was a richer country than China and continued to be so for centuries. Here, it needs mention that established Indian scholars have developed the habit of trespassing the area of the darkness of their knowledge, and Amartya Sen is no exception.

So far the spread of Buddhism in China is concerned; it was the joint effort of the Indian and Central Asian–Parthian,

Khotanese, Sogdian/Kang, Kuchean/Tocharians/Yuch-chi, etc. Buddhist savants. The Central Asians role in exporting Indian music and musical instruments to China is equally well known. The Chinese continued to be a lesser power in the early years of Common Era. They were late comers in the region, as its first exploratory mission, the mission led by Chang-Chien, came to Central Asia only in 128 B.C.

As mentioned above India was not only a soft power. At the beginning of the Common Era(CA), according to the noted economic historian Angus Madison, when the, GDP of the world was $102.5 billions (at 1990 international $), India, was the largest contributor to the global economy with $33.75 billions. China followed India with $26.83. In percentage term, it was 32.9% and 26.9% respectively. The data for other regions given in the brackets, such as total Western Europe(10.8%), Eastern Europe (1.9%), former USSR (1.5%). Other Asia (16.1%), clearly indicates that India was not only ahead in the field of religion and culture its economic dominance also continued at least for the next 1700 years with India's share of 28.9% during 1000 CA (China 22.7%). 24.5% during 1500 CA (China 25%) and 24.4% during 1700 CA (China, 22.3%) till it collapsed due to British colonial rule to 4.2% with China's 4.5% during, 1950 Under such situation, the stronger pull and the direction of the trade and commerce in those days was towards north-south. Moreover, silk was an item of diplomacy for the Chinese, rather than the item of trade; as such the nomenclature 'Silp Route' is a misnomer. In reality, it was the '*Sutra* Route'. The book discusses many such misconceptions and myths.

B.B. Kumar

Acknowledgements

India' relations with its neighbours has always interested me. This knowledge makes the self-portrait of India clearer. My numerous discussions with Professor Lokesh Chandra about our relationship with the neighbours, especially with Central Asia, used to be highly refreshing; it brought clarity. I am grateful to him for the moments spared and shared with me.

I also thank him for writing the foreword of the book. Padma Bhushan K. Santhanam has kindly written the introduction of the book. I thank him for sparing his valuable time and doing the same. I have published papers of Central Asian and Indian scholars in the two special numbers of the Dialogue and its other issues. My discussions with them have always been helpful for me. At this moment, I remember many of them, especially, Professor Devendra Kaushik, Dr. S.P. Gupta, Shri K. Santhanam, Professor Surat Mirkasymov, Professor R.G. Gidadhubli, Professor P.L. Dash, Professor R.R. Sharma, Dr, S.S. Toshkhani, Shri J.N. Roy, Dr. Evgeny Kablukov, Dr. M.Kh. Abuseitova, Professor Nirmala Joshi, Dr. Ramakant Dwivedi and many others. At this moment, I remember and thank them.

My study and writings often deprive my wife Shail, children – Pranav, Ajit and Utpal – and daughters-in-laws Babita, Rakhi and Chandra – and the grand children Yash, Shreya and Jayant of my time. I affectionately remember them at this hour.

Last, but not the least, I remember and thank my publisher Shri Ashok K. Mittal of Concept Publishing Company Pvt. Ltd. for taking utmost interest and meticulous care in publishing this book, as he did earlier.

B.B. Kumar

Contents

1

India and Central Asia : Links and Interactions

India and Central Asia, with common and contiguous borders, climatic continuity, similar geographical features and geo-cultural affinity, have long traditions of socio-cultural, political and economic contacts since remote past. Their relations have been multi-dimensional, deep, old and continuous There has been uninterrupted flow of men, material and the ideas between the two. The Indian and foreign literary sources attest to the fact. According to *Zend Avesta,* the ancestors of Iranian, Indian and Turanian people were the three sons of Tratoria, namely Arya, Sairimia and Tura respectively.[1] Abu Qasim Farishta gives a very interesting account of the geneology of the Indians and the Central Asians.[2]

The excavations in Southern Uzbekistan in the Amu Darya valley, in Afrasiab in the north-eastern edge of Samarkand and elsewhere in Uzbekistan, in Turkmenistan, Kazakhstan and in the Tak-mak region of Kyrghyzstan provide ample proof of Indo-Central Asian links from ancient days. Extensive excavations have been done with remarkable findings at Kara Tepa, Fayaz Tepa, Dalverzin Tepa, Yer Kurgan, Ak-Beshin, Kranayerezka and Isyk-Ata. Sakas, Kushanas, Hunas, Turks and Mughals came from Central Asia to India. India had very intimate historic, cultural links with eastern Central Asian regions of Xinjiang and Tibet also. Findings of the excavations and the discovery of manuscripts in Xinjiang and Tibetan literary documents provide enough material to establish our links. India had rulers of Central Asian origin. Dynasties of Indian origin ruled Khotan and elsewhere in Central Asia.

Ancient Links

Ancient Indo-Central Asia links were well established. The leading pre-historians of Russia have discovered large remains of Sohan Culture across the difficult moutainous terrain of the Hindukush and the Pamirs in the valley of Oxus and its tributaries in Tajikistan, Kazakhstan and other places. The discoveries by V. Ranov, Kh. A. Alphasbayev and others in Soviet journals provide enough light on this subject. The first stage of Old Stone Age or Palaeolithic culture of Central Asia was named Borykazghan culture after the typesize in southern Kazakhstan. Ranov named it Soan culture of Central Asia. Diffusion of culture continued in the Neolithic stage and in Bronze Age culture also. There is marked similarity in Kangra valley neolithic culture of India and Gissan (Hissar) culture of Central Asia. Altin Depe, Khapuz Depe, Namazga Depe Tahirbai Depe, Anau, etc. in south Turkmenistan bear unmistakable stamp of Indus civilization.[3] T. Shirinov, in a paper presented in a seminar on "India and Central Asia" (Pre-Islamic period) "held in Tashkent in the year 2000 on the subject "Contact between Central Asia and the Indian subcontinent in the second millennium B.C." has pointed out that "Cultural and trading relations between Central Asia and the Indian subcontinent in the third to second millennium B.C. were closer than they are described by many contemporary researchers".

Central Asia was well known during the epic age. Indian epics (*Ramayana* and *Mahabharata*) and the *Purāṇas* have numerous references of the region, its topography, mountains, rivers and the people. Many communities of Central Asia participated in *Mahabharata* war. Shakas and Yavanas (Greeks) have been described as degraded *Kshatriyas* by the *Mahabharata* and *Manu Smṛti* (Hindu code). There is mention of Shakas, Pahlavas (Persians), Kambojas (Galcha speaking people of Tazikistan), Rishik (Yueh-chi or Kushanas) at one place in the *Mahabharata* (5.4.15). At another place, China, Huna and Shaka are mentioned (*Mahabharata* 2.47.19). Kanka (Kangyu of Sogd) are mentioned with Shaka and Tushara (Tokharian). Enough material on Central Asia is available in Medieval Sanskrit literature, and in Buddhist and Jain literatures.

Parts of India and Central Asia were ruled together during Ashokan, Achaemenian, Seleucid and Kushana periods. The use of Indian languages and scripts, Buddhism, Hinduism and Islam, rule of dynasties of Indian origin in many kingdoms of Central Asia and that of the dynasties of Central Asian origin in India further deepened their links. The ruins of the Buddhist monasteries of the period from 525 B.C. to 700 A.D. have been found in Transoxiana.[4]

Two names figure prominently in the spread of Buddhism in Central Asia. They are of Ashoka and Kanishka. Pentti Aalto has mentioned[5] about an inscription on the wall of the gate of Chuyung-Kuan, a town on the road from Peking to Kalgan in Sanskrit, Tibetan, Hsi-hsia, Uigur, Mongol and Chinese languages, which reads: "The great and illustrious Cakravarti King Ashoka, having assembled the relics of Lord Buddha of great virtue, adorned beautifully the vast world with *stupas,* and made the great *Dharma* shine greatly throughout the world". Kandhar inscriptions of 258 B.C. in Greek and Aramaic says that as a result of Ashoka's activity, "everything prospers over the whole earth". Kanishka patronized Buddhism. According to Chinese tradition, it is said that Lord Buddha understood Kanishka's Yueh-chi language.[6]

According to the ancient Khotanese tradition, the kingdom of Khotan was established by Kutsan, the son of Ashoka in 240 B.C. There is yet one other tradition which says that Khotan was founded by exiled Gandharan subjects of Ashoka. Language of the documents discovered in various archaeological expeditions of Khotan in Chinese Turkistan was Prakrit. It is the Gandharan dialect of Middle Indo-Aryan. The documents known as Kharoshthi documents are written in Kharoshthi script of India. Apart from the manuscript of Dharmapada, the documents have enough secular materials written on wood, leather and silk found at Loulan (Kroraina). These facts give credence to the tradition of Gandhara expansion to Turkistan.[7] In this connection, it needs mention that several dynasties of Central Asian states claimed Indian origin. Apart from the Vijaya rulers of Khotan, in the south there were many others, such as Pushpa and Deva ending rulers at Kucha, and those with Arjuna suffix at Karasahr (Agnidesha) in the north with Sanskrit/Indian names. Names, such as Anand, Buddhamitra, Dharmapala, Punyadeva, and Vasudeva; regal titles, such as *maharaja* (great king), *rajatiraja, avijitasimha* (unconquered lion); and sometimes, mixed names, such as Vasu Mogiya, Vasu Kekeya, etc., in the records were indicative of Indian links[8].

Indo-Central-Asian interaction was most intimate during the Kushana period. However, the same continued even after that.

Frescoes reminiscent of Bharhut and Ajanta caves has come to light in the excavations of Penjikent (Tajikistan), Varaksha (Uzbekistan) and Azhina Tepe (Tajikistan). A fresco carrying the painting of a blue dancer wearing tiger skin with a trident in the background at Penjikent is identified with Śiva, the Nilakantha (blue necked). A painting on the palace-wall at Varaksha shows a king hunting a tiger riding on elephant back along with his retenue. At Adina Tepe, a figure of sleeping Buddha (about 12 metre size) in *Nirvana* posture is found. These finds clearly show the influence of Indian tradition. A painted figure, supposed to be of a worshipper or of Indra, seems distinctly Indian in structure, colouring, costumes and style similar to some Ajanta figures.[9] Excavations have brought to light the existence of numerous Buddhist temples and caves with icons, paintings in Central Asia with Indian influences. But Central Asia has also assimilated diverse elements from other sources. Local elements and adaptations are also not lacking.

An outstanding Buddha figure in Balawaste shows some significant non-Buddhist symbols like sun, moon, flaming jewels, etc. These were originally used in Hindu iconography and developed Tantric symbolism later on. The *shrivasta* mark, originally meant for Viṣṇu, was seen in the centre of the Buddha's chest. In other case, there was depiction of the *samudrāmanthana* legend. Most of the paintings from Dandan Uiliq, Balawaste and Farhad-Beg-Yailaki sites of Domoko region of Khotan oasis had Mahayana Buddhist themes, but some popular Hindu divine figures were also depicted on them.[10] Kucha, an important seat of Hinayana Buddhism, reflected best of the Indian traditions in painting. The first out of the styles of the paintings clearly shows the influence of the Gandhara and Gupta traditions. Kizil cave paintings remind us of the Ajanta traditions. Indian elements in the art of Kizil is more prominently shown. The figure of Gopala with cows from the Cave of the Statues, the figure of Dilip as described in Kalidasa's *Raghuvamsha,* the graceful dance depiction of queen Chandra-prabha shows it amply. The Ajanta style is clearly seen in the last one.[11] The theme is a Hindu one. The Indian motifs like lotus, multi-limbed divinities, e.g. a thousand multiple eyes (*Sahasraksha*) on the body of Avalokiteshvara in certain silk paintings of Tun-Huang, may be cited as examples. In the cave of Thousand Buddhas at Tun-Huang, the artists painted the walls and the ceilings of the caves depicting scenes from the life of the Buddha, stories of the

Jatakas and Bodhisattvas, as well as various Hindu gods and goddesses, like Śiva and Ganesha.[12]

Buddhism was introduced in Khotan by the king Vijayasambhava under the spiritual guidance of Arya Vairochana. The first monastery was established there in 211 B.C. The religion spread to other southern states from there. Marco Polo visited Sachiu in this region and found that people were "for the most part idolators". Fa-Hien, travelling in the region during 399-414 A.D., found that all the inhabitants of the Khotan region "professed Buddhist law, and joined together in its religious musk for their enjoyment". Hiuen Chwang also confirmed the fact. Fa-Hien was lodged in a monastery in Khotan where three thousand monks stayed. It was known as Gomati monastery. There were four great monasteries and many smaller ones there according to Fa-Hien.[13]

Buddhism had deep roots in northern Xinjiang (Chinese Turkistan), specially in the states of Kucha, Karashahr (Agnidesha), Turfan (Kaochang) and Bharuka (Aksu). Kucha was an important Buddhist centre since first century A.D. It played important role in the propagation of Buddhism. Famous Buddhist scholar, Kumarajiva was the son of a Kuchian mother and Indian father. Balkh was an important centre of Buddhist sites and was known as 'Little Rajagriha'. The places around it had numerous *sangharams,* and statues of Buddha. It had a hundred convents and five hundred monks. There was a convent called *Navasangharama* outside the city. A former ruler built it. There was a figure of Buddha studded with gems. The hall was also well-decorated with the same. It was often raided and plundered by the covetous neighbouring rulers. It had also a statue of Pishamen (Vaisravana) and it was believed that he protects the precincts of the convent. Tirmiz and Aksu each had ten *sangharamas* and a thousand monks. Chaghaniyan, Kubadian, Sumana and Kulab had few *sangharamas* and monks each. Northern Xinjiang had the followers of Hinayana sect.[14]

Buddhist links with Xinjiang are well-known. Buddhist and Hindu icons have been found in Buddhist temples of Khotan, Kucha, Dandan Uiliq and other places. Buddhist and Hindu links in western Central Asia, as stated earlier, has also come to light after excavations by Soviet archaeologists.[15] The central regions of the western Central Asia was especially rich in art and architecture. This region, known as Sogdiana had multi-layered links with India.

R.H. Sulemanov, in a paper presented in a seminar held in Tashkent in 2000 A.D. on "India and Central Asia (Pre-Islamic period)" has brought out many Indian parallels in ancient cults of Sogdiana. He has specially mentioned about the funeral rites among the tribes and the same in Vedic tradition, the cult of fire worship and Mithraism (Sun worship; Mithra/Mitra is Vedic Sun god, Iranian word is Mihir), the legend of Gandharvas (water deities) and the Ganges. Place names such as Kanka or Ganga has also the Central Asian connections. *Mahabharata* mentions the name of Kanka (Kangyu tribe). The water deity was also worshipped in Central Asia as perfect women.[16]

Apart from the Puranic cults mentioned above, the worship of five Hindu gods in Sogdiana, namely Brahma, Indra, Mahadeva (Śiva), Nārāyaṇa and Vaishravana needs special mention. Brahma, Indra and Śiva had the Sogdian names of Zravan, Adbad and Veshparkar respectively. The four armed goddess riding the lion may be Durga.[17] Portable fire altars associated with Mahadeva-Veshparkar, Brahma-Zravan and Indra-Abdab found in a mural of eighth century at Penjikent also needs special mention. It may also be mentioned that the name of Iranian supreme god Ahur Mazda in this case,[18] and that of Iranian river goddess Anahita Harahwati Ardavisura in the case metioned above is not used in Central Asia. Russian scholars have related three or four armed deities in west Central Asian murals, Hindu and Buddhist God Vishwakarma (creator of everything; Sanskrit) and a case of an obvious transformation of Indian cults.[19]

A fragment of Kharoshti inscription discovered by Russian scholar A.N. Burnshtan in Tajikistan, and translated by J. Harmatta, is attributed to the second-first century B.C. on paleographic grounds. It teads: 'Nārāyaṇa, be victorious'. Paintings of Śiva from various sites of eastern and western Central Asia, and that of the Gaṇeś, Kumār/Kārtikeya, Mahākālā, Durgā, Digpālas and of Vishwarūpa Kṛṣṇa at various places of Central Asia confirm Hindu linkages.[20]

God Śiva appears on certain coins of Gondophares, Maues and several other kings who ruled Central Asia and India. The coins of Kushana rulers also have Śiva with his consort Umā and the son Kārtikeya-Kumāra. Vima owed personal allegiance to Śiva.

Ancient Land Routes

India and Central Asia were linked through many land routes. The Indian traders, at the close of 1880s, started bringing goods to Central Asia through Persia. This new trade route was less dangerous and cheaper. They asked for and received permission from the Russian authorities to use even a more advantageous route to Central Asia after the construction of trans-Caspian railway. The route was from Bombay port to Black Sea port of Batumi and then across Caucasus to Central Asia.[21] Takshashila and Purushpura on either side of the Sindhu river were connected with Indian trade routes on Indian side and Central Asian trade routes on the other. Strategically located, Takshashila, the capital city of Gandhar, was the terminus of several major inland routes and the starting point of the great trade routes connecting India and Central Asia. A route towards the north passing through Kashmir valley to Gilgit, Yarkand and Kashgarh connected it to eastern and western Turkistan. The western route passed through Pushkalavati, Purushpura (Peshawar) and Kapisha (modern Begram) to Bactria. The route from Kapisha to Bactria ran through Bamiyan and number of passes – Robat, Dandan, Shikan and Karakotal; followed Dana Yousouf river route to reach Mazar-i-Sarif and then Bactria. It was the oldest and most frequented route. Hiuen Tsang reached Bactria from Samarkand and then followed this route to reach Bamiyan, Kapisha and Purushpura through Khaibar pass. Bactria became very important as natural converging point of several routes. Babylon, Susa-Herat, Samarkand-Tashkent in the Oxus valley in the north, and a number of routes from Kashgarh in the west. The importance of Takshashila-Kapisha-Bactria route increased during Achaemenian period when Punjab was its satrapi and during Seleucid period when it became royal highway to the west. Two routes connected Bactria to the Oxus valley. Strabo, Pliny and other geographers have mentioned about Caspian Highway going towards the Caspian Sea. Indians favoured this route for trade to the Black Sea ports taking advantage of the navigability of Oxus river. The route to Tashkent *via* Samarkand went farther to the north-east to Turfan. Tashkent-Turfan route passed through the northern parts of Tien Shan range and through Kulja and Uranchi cities. Khojend lies about 150 miles south-east of Tashkent.[22] Alexander suffered a military disaster

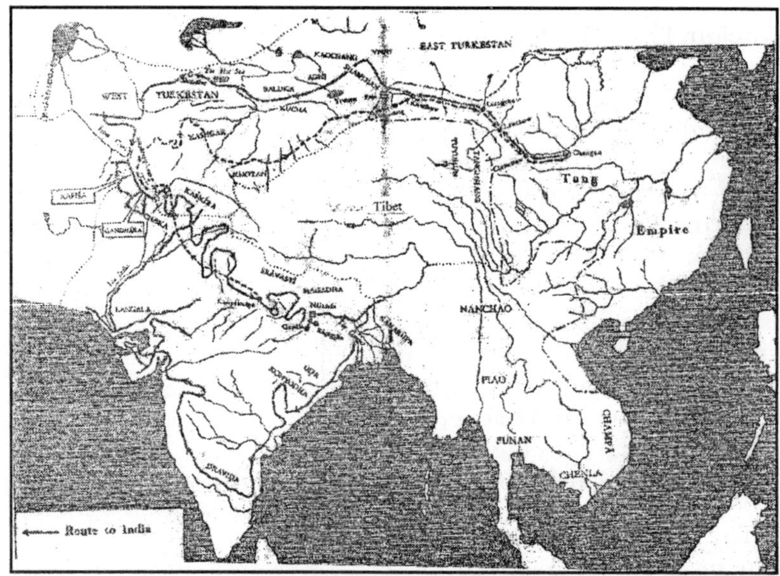

Hiuen-Tsang's Route to India

while passing through Smarkand or Marchanda. He went up to Khojend, known as Alexandria Eschate (farthest) at that time.[23]

Kashgarh, on the western fringe of the Taklamakan desert in Tarim basin, in between the Tien Shan range on the north and Kun-lun mountain range in the south, was on farther west, which became prominent due to the development of the silk route and silk trade. Two routes emerging from Kashgarh passed though the important places located in the series of oases on the outer periphery of the oval shaped trough-like Tarim basin desert. Imortant places, like Yarkand, Karghalik, Keriya, Niya, Endere, Charchan, Charkhlik and Miran, and after skirting the salty Lop-nor marsh, Tun-huang and An-hsi were located on the southern route. It passed through the southern periphery of the desert on the northern foot-hills of Kun-lun. The northern route, on the northern periphery south of Tien Shan, passed through Uch-Turfan, Aksu, Kucha and Korla. There was bifurcation of the route at Korla towards south-east and north-east. The south-eastern route passed through Kuruk Darya, Lou-lan, etc. and terminated at Tung-huang. Karashahr and Turfan were located on north-eastern route. The route made a great arch through Hami, and then ended at An-hsi. Tashkent-Kulja-Urunchi route met Akshu-Kucha-Karashahr route at Turfan. Hiuen Tsang followed Hami-Turfan-Tashkent-Samarkand road, descended from Oxus valley to Bactria, and then reached Purushpura in India through Bamiyan-Kapisha-Purushpura route. An alternative route links India to Kashgarh *via* Bactria through a route passing south of Pamir. Hiuen Tsang in 644 A.D. for his return journey to China and *Marco Polo* for his journey to Cathay in 1273 A.D. used the same. Passing from Bactria to Badakhshan up to the open valley of Wakhan, it goes to Sariqol south of the peak Muz Tagh Ata, and then to Tashkurghan and finally, descending the hills to the Kashgarh and Yarkand. A route from Kashmir valley through Gilgit, Darkot and Baroghil passes meets Badakhshan-Wakhan-Sariqol route at Sarhad.[24]

Central Asia in Ancient Indian Literature

The Indian epics and *Purāṇas* mention about the earth consisting of seven *dvipas,* the number varies in some cases. *Dvipa,* ordinarily, means island. Paṇini derives it from *dvi + ap,* meaning 'land between two arms of water'.[25] However, the Puranic *dvipas* stand for continents or tribal or national territories.[26] It signified all types of natural or human regions — big or small.[27] The barriers may be water, sand, swamp, high mountains or thick forests.[28] Jambudvipa is at the centre of all. Mount Meru is at the centre of the Jambudvipa. It needs mention that India and Central Asia form part of the Jambudvipa. Mount Meru is the Pamir knot.

Details of the mountains, rivers, vegetation, climate, etc of the *dvipas* have been given in most of the *Purāṇas,* and some scholars tried to identify specific geographical region basing on the same. Al-Beruni, as for example, located Pushkardvipa between Cina and Mangala (perhaps China and Mongolia).[29] Jambudvipa, also known as Sudarshandvipa, is said to be circular in shape[30] and surrounded by the sea in all the sides. It has six mountain ranges — Himalaya, Hemakuta, Nishadha, Nila, Sveta and Shringavat[31] — and nine zones (*varshas*) – Hari, Bhadrashva, Ketumal, Bharata, Uttar-Kuru, Sweta, Hiranyaka, Airavata and Ilavrita.[32] According to the *Markandeya Purāṇa,* Jambudvipa is depressed on the south and north and elevated and broad in the middle.[33] The elevated region is known Ilavrita or Meruvarsha; mountain Meru is at the centre of the same.

The nine divisions of Jambudvipa according to different *Purāṇas*, such as *Matsya Purāṇa* are: Ilavrita, Ramyaka or Ramanaka, Hiranmaya or Hiranyaka, Uttara-Kuru or Shringashaka, Bhadrashva, Ketumal, Hari, Kimpurusha and Bharata.[34] The first division, as mentioned above, is centrally located, the next three and the last three in the north and south respectively, and the remaining two, Bhadrashva and Ketumala to the east and west respectively. The geographical detail of the region is given in the *Mahabharata's Bhishma parva* in detail and in other *Purāṇas* also. *Markandeya*[35] and *Brahmand Purāṇas*[36] divide Jambudvipa into four regions shaped like four petals of a lotus. Four rivers flow from Mount Meru, namely Sita, flowing to the east through mountains to the Badrashva region to the sea; Alakananda flowing to the south through India to the sea; Chakshu (or Vakshu or Oxus) flowing through the mountains towards west to the Ketumala region, and Bhadra flowing through northern mountains and Uttar Kuru region to the sea.[37]

Vayu Purāṇa details the mountain ranges, valleys river systems, etc. of the geographical region of Jambudvipa making it possible to identify some of their geographical features. The description of the northern regions of Jambudvipa, according to S.M. Ali, 'covers a very vast area, from the Urals and the Caspian to the Yenisel and from the 'Turkestan, Tien Shan ranges to the Arctic. It describes topography of the whole land very accurately and in some cases picturesquely ....'[38] Bhadrashva, in the east, is identical with the basins of Tarim and Hwangho rivers, i.e., the whole of Singkiang and northern China'.[39] Ketumala to the west of Meru, through which river Chakshu (Oxus) flows, corresponds to western Turkestan.[40] It is believed to cover 'practically the whole of the ancient Bactria which included the whole of the present Afghan Turkistan (north of Hindukush), the lower Harirud valley, the basin of Murkhab Kashka system (all south of the old bed of Amu Darya) and the basins of the Surkhan, Kafirnigan, Vakhsh and Yaksu rivers...'[41] Hari[42] and Bharata represented western Tibet and India respectively. The area around Meru, the mountainous region, was Meruvarsha or Ilavrita. The area across the Himalayas and Hindukush from Pamir up to Arctic was known as Uttar Kuru. Arctic was known as Somagiri.[43] There is numerous mention of the region in the *Ramayana* and the *Mahabharata*, the two Indian epics.

Valmiki, in the *Ramayana*, gives graphic picture of Uttar Kuru and Somagiri.[44] Sugriva, while sending the monkeys to the north for searching Sita, describes the route and the countries in that direction. Among others, he commands them to search Sita in the lands and towns of the Dardas, Kambojas, Yavanas and Shakas.[45] He describes Uttar Kuru and Somagiri (the Arctic region). There is the sea and the Somagiri in the extreme north. The route is extremely difficult one. The region is without the sun and yet very much lighted. There are no national boundaries there.[46] Arjuna brought water from the northern sea for the coronation of Yudhisthira.[47]

Mahabharata describes Meru (Pamir), Meruvarsha around it, Ketumala to its east, and Uttar Kuru to its north.[48] Meru, according to the Indian classical literature, is located at the centre of the earth. The conference of the *Devas* (gods) was held at Mount Meru to decide about the churning of the sea.[49]

Central Asian People in Indian Classical Literature

There is numerous mention of the people of the Central Asia in Indian literature, especially in the *Ramayana,* as stated above, and the *Mahabharata* and the *Purāṇas.* Shaka, Darada, Pahlava, Kirata and Parada are said to be *Kshatriyas* of good birth.[50] It was suggested to invite Shaka, Pahlava, Rishik and Darada kings in the *Mahabharata* war from Pandava side.[51] *Mahabharata* mentions that Arjuna brought tribute from Uttara Kuru[52] and another Pandava hero, Nakula defeated Hunas, Pahalvas, Yavanas and Shakas.[53] Yudhisthira received tribute from Uttar Kuru.[54] Shakas, Hunas and Tusharas also paid tribute to him.[55] It needs mention that Tusharas are also known as Yueh-chi (in Chinese language) and Kanishka belonged to that community. Tusharas were present in the *Rajasuya Yajna* of Yudhisthira.[56] They participated in *Mahabharata* war from the Kaurava side.[57] They were ferocious warriors.[58] The name of Tushara-Giri (Tushara mountain) finds mention in *Mahabharata, Harshacharita* and *Kavyamimamsa.*[59] Chakshu river (Oxus or Amu Darya) flows through Tushara, Lampak, Pahlava, Parada and Shaka countries, according to the *Vayu Purāṇa* and *Matsya Purāṇa.*[60] It shows that these countries belonged to the Central Asia.

India's contact with Central Asia is ancient one. The inhabitants of Uttar Kuru seem to be legendary fellows in the epics and later literature, but as historic ones in the *Aitareya Brahmana* according to the author of Vedic Index. Uttar Kuru is the Divine land (region of Devas) for Vasistha Satya Havya, but Atyarati wants to conquer it.[61] Indians remember Jambudvipa during their daily worship which includes Central Asia.[62]

Immigration of the people from Central Asia to India is a well-known fact of history. Shakas, Yavanas Hunas, Turks, Mongols and Pathans came to India. Most of the immigrants were absorbed in Indian society. Yavanas and the Maga Brahmanas came from the north-west. Patanjali's *Mahabhashya* and *Gargi Samhita* echo frequent incursion of the Greek chiefs from Bactria to India. Varahamihira, the famous astronomer, was a Maga Brāhmīn.[63] Here, it needs mention that Indian tradition, says about out-migration of Shakas, Yavanas, etc. from India.

Sagara was an ancient Indian king. His father was defeated and humiliated by some *Kshatriyas.* He was forced to live as an ascetic in the forest. Sagar regained his kingdom in due course and wanted to take revenge and kill his enemies. His priest Vashistha intervened to save their lives. He persuaded Sagara to spare them. They were forced to abandon their religiously ordained duty and declared dead while living (*Jivanmṛita,* a man abandoning his ordained duties and considered dead while living). Brahmana priests abandoned them as they stopped performing their religious duties. They were degraded socially; became *Vrishal/Vratya/Shudra/Kshatriya Shudra.* Sagara killed Haihayas and Talajangha Kshatriyas. Shakas, Yavanas, Kambojas, Pardas and Pahlavas became Vrishala (*Kshatriya Shudras*)[64] According to *Mahabharata,* Shakas, Yavanas, Kambojas and Mahashakas were *Kshatriyas.* They became Vrishala due to not availing the benefits of the contact of the Brahmanas.[65] Lack of proper conduct is also said to be the reason for such degradation for Tushara and others.[66] Anushasan Parva of *Mahabharata,* further says that some, *Kshatriya* communities — Mekal, Dravida, Lat, Paundra, Kanvashira, Darad, Darva, Chaur, Shabar, Barber, Kirat, and Yavana — were degraded due to their envy for the Brahmanas.[67] *Manu Smṛti* regards Shakas, Yavanas, as degraded *Kshatriyas* reduced to the status of Vrishalas.[68]

According to Sagara legend mentioned above, Shakas, Yavanas, Kambojas, Pardas and Pahlavas were the inhabitants of India. In historic time, they were mostly settled in the Central Asia and the countries west of India. This phenomenon presupposes their out-migration from India. Patanjali, in his *Mahabhashya,* considers Shakas, and Yavanas to be the migrants from India.[69]

As discussed above, considerable geographical information about India and its neighbourhood in Central Asia is available in the *Purāṇas* and the Indian epics. The same is the case with medieval Indian literature. *Kavyamimamsa* of Rajshekhara, Kalhan's *Rajatarangini,* some lexicons, Sanskrit and Buddhist prose narratives and fables, etc. provide valuable information in this direction. Gunadhya's *Brihatkatha,* Somdeva's *Katha-Saritsagar,* Kshemendra's *Brihat-Katha-Manjari* and its Jaina adaptation, *Vasudeva-Hindi* provide valuable information and insight for understanding the geography and other information about India and its neighbourhood. Kalidasa's epics and dramas provide graphic picture of the northern mountain region of India. This is especially so in the case of *Meghdoota,* and *Vikramorvashiam.* He brings refreshing reference of Uttar Kuru.

The fables and narratives in the books mentioned above provide valuable information based on the experiences of the travellers. It needs mention that Central Asia was frequently visited by Indian traders, monks and scholars. Ruling dynasties, such as that of Khotan claimed Indian origin. Shakas, Hunas, Kushanas of Central Asian origin ruled parts of India. Monarchs of Turk and Mongol origin ruled India and continued to have Central Asian links to some extent. The knowledge about the region was reflected in the classical and medieval literature of India. In this connection, it needs mention that perceptional haziness has developed due to frequent changes in the names of regions, places, mountains, rivers and the people. There have been shifting frontiers. One group of people have often replaced the others. However, many names, items of trade, the geographical features, etc. have not changed considerably; Kubha, Gomati, Vakshu and Gandhar have become Kabul, Gomal, Oxus and Kandahar. The community names of Shaka, Huna, Kushana have not changed. The items presented to the *Mahabharata* hero/monarch Yudhisthira are still known to be produced in the region. This has led many scholars to identify the names of the Central Asia and correlate them with those mentioned in the Indian literature.

Tashkent, the capital city of Uzbekistan, and Samarkand, the ancient capital of Sogdiana and that of Timur and Babar, are ancient cities. The old name of Tashkent is Chach. Pulleyblank wanted to connect it with Yenisseian word for 'stone': Ket. *Tyes*, Kot, *shish*, Pumpokolsk *cys*. He sees it as a relic of the Huna occupation of the Sogdiana in the fifth and sixth centuries. However, as the word finds place in the inscriptions of Shapur I (240-272 A.D.) and therefore, it had earlier currency. In the old Chinese records, Tashkent is transcribed with the hieroglyph '*shih*' that is stone. The name is linked with Turkic *tash*, 'stone' and may be considered a translation of the older names of the city. It is pointed out that the older names of the city before '*Chach*' also had the meaning 'stone'. The inhabitants of the area, according to Chinese sources were *Ch'iang chu* or *K'ang çhu*, very likely of Tukharian origin. *K'ang* may mean some kind of stone in Tokharian. In Hindi, '*kankar* is pebble. According to *Sutralaṁkāra*, a painter of Pushkalawati visited the country *Ashmaka* (meaning stone or stoney) and out of his piety decorated a Buddhist monastery. The place is identified with Tashkent. There was a tradition that *Sutrālaṁkāra* was written by Ashvaghosha. Others attribute its authorship to Kumarlat, the founder of *Sautrantika* school of Buddhism. Ashmak, was the name of a north-western country, according to the *Brihatsaṁhitā* of Varahamihira. Kumarajiva knew the great cities of the North like Alasanda and Tashkent.[70] It needs mention that the word *Tashkent* first appears in *Ta'rikh al-Hind* of al-Beruni.[71]

The name *Kanka* appears in *Mahabharata* with the names of other tribes of Central Asia. It is the same as *Kang* mentioned earlier. At one place, it comes with Shakas and Tusharas (*Shakas tusharah kankascha; Mahabharata*)[72] At another place, it comes with Shakas, Tusharas and Pahlavas (*shakas tusharah kankashch pahlavashcha.*[73] *Kankas* are mentioned twice in *Bhagawata Purāṇa,* together with the Kiratas, Hunas, Andhras, Pulindas, Pukkasas, Abhiras, Yavanas and Khasas;[74] and then again with Kiratas, Hunas, Yavanas, Andhras, Khasas and Shakas.[75] A point which needs to be kept in mind here is that the names of the neighbouring communities are often clubbed together in the classical Indian literature. However, this is not done if the social factor, such as the mobility in the social frame, is discussed.

Panini in his *Ashtadhyayi* has mentioned the word *kantha*. The word in *Kashika Sutra* denotes 'town' or 'city'. The 'kand' or 'kent'of Tashkent, Samarkand, Yarkand, etc is the same as the above-mentioned *kantha.* Tashkent and Yarkand, I am told, were also known as 'Dakshikantha' and 'Yahvarkantha' respectively. The Sanskrit word for 'Turk' is *Turushka.* The first syllable of the name is found in the name of 'Turvasu' in classical Indian literature. The second syllable 'shka' is a superlative suffix found in the name of Kanishka; the meaning of 'Kanishka' is the youngest son.[76]

The last syllable of the Central Asian nations is 'stan'. It is related to the Sanskrit 'sthan' and Persian 'stan', denoting land or place. Kasyapa was a seer and progenitor of the living world according to the Indian mythology. Phrigia is called Phrugia in Greek. Indian literature has Bhrigu, a seer. I am not sure whether 'Phoenic' of the word 'Phoenician' can be derived from Semitic roots. Sanskrit has the word "Banik', the traders. I feel the deep study of the languages and cultures of Central Asia may help Indians in understanding themselves better. The reverse may be equally true.

Contacts during Medieval and Modern Period

Indians pleasantly remember Mirza Abdul Rahim Khan-e-Khana and Mirza Ghalib. The former was an eminent Hindi poet. He was a Turkmen. His father Bairam Khan was the tutor-guardian of the Mughal Emperor Akbar. Mirza Ghalib was an eminent Urdu poet. When we remember Central Asia, we lovingly remember both of them. Both had their roots in Central Asia. Babar, the founder of Mughal dynasty in India was the ruler of this area. Some Sultans were scions of the Turkmen, Khilji and Tughlak tribes. Babar, the founder of the Mughal dynasty in India was the king of Farghana in Central Asia. The number of *manasabdars* (high ranking nobles) in Delhi Sultanate and Mughal courts was very large. During first hundred years of the Delhi Sultanate, the immigrant groups, such as the Turks, Khiljis, Ghurids and Tajiks maintained very strong grip on power. As much as fifty per cent of the appointments made on the accession of Muhammad-bin-Tughlaq was from among the amirs of Khurasan, which included Turks, natives of Mongolia and Persia. Several hundred people from Central Asia came to India with Babar. The nobility comprised mainly of Turanis (Central Asians) with a sprinkling of Persians (Iranis). The number of the Iranis increased in the nobility of Humayun, the son of Babar after his exile in the Safavid court. Fiftyseven nobles accompanied

Humayun to India, of which 27 were Turanis, 21 were Iranis and nine remained unidentified.[77] Turani stranglehold weakened during Akbar's rule when the Turani nobles revolted against him.[78]

The people from the Central Asia migrated to India due to various reasons. Delhi Sultanate and Mughal court patronized Muslim scholars, artists, soldiers and Sufi saints from Central Asia, Iran and the Arab countries. A galaxy of scholars and men of fine arts had clustered at the Mughal court. There was large exodus to India whenever the economic and political conditions deteriorated in Central Asia. Mention is made of 15 luminaries in Mughal court, namely Jalali Kitobar, Dasturi Nasafi, Khwaja Sami Sadat, Ghubar, Mulla, Mustafidi Balkhi, Munim Bukhari, Mustaidi Bukhari, and others. There is mention of 274 poets from Bukhara, Samarkand, Nasaf, Badakhshan and other places migrating to India.[79] Turanis were preferred as guards or watchmen (*pasbani*) and warriors. Turani soldiers received twice the amount in comparison of the Indians. It was easier for the refugee infiltrators to get such jobs.[80] There used to be massive migration from Central Asia during natural calamities. It is reported that 12,000 people fled to India during 1730s when there was severe famine in Transoxiana. The people also left for India due to political disturbances, anarchy or tyranny.[81] People fled/immigrated to other countries from Balkh during the tyranic rule of Muhammed Bi. Many left their homes for India during the invasion of Bulkh by Abdullah Khan.[82]

The visit of scholars and Sufi saints from Central Asia to India is a well-known phenomena. Al-Beruni and Abdurazzak Samarkandi came to India from Khwarezm. Central Asian scholars, Al-Khwarezmi and Ibn-e-Sina were aware of the works of Indian scholars, Aryabhatta on Mathematics and Astronomy, and that of Charak and Susrut through their Arabic translations. Many Muslim Sufi saints came from Central Asian cities of Bukhara and Samarkand. Poets from Bukhara and Merv stayed at the imperial court of Akbar. Khwaja Parsa, Makhfi, Mirza Sirajuddin, Furqat, Hamza Hakim Zadeh and other poets came from Central Asia to India even in the nineteenth century. Tajjali Hindi, Agha Munir went from India. Poets like Nasim, Nasafi, Maharam, Mushrib and Shaukat popularized Indian style of poetry in Central Asia. A group of learned men in Khwarezm were engaged in the translation of Indian historical and literary works in Uzbeg language. Some translations, like that of Aryabhatta's *Ardharatrika* is available even now.[83]

Al-Beruni and Al-Khwarezmi were two scholars from Transoxiana, Central Asia. They perfected Sanskrit and Indian Sciences. Al-Beruni's 'Tarikh-ul-Hind' provides encyclopaedic information about India. Al-Khwarezmi was highly interested in Indian mathematics; he produced an excellent astronomical 'Zij' based on Hindu parameters and methods of calculations. His works on Indian astronomy and mathematics were translated from Arabic to Latin in 1126 A.D. It was entitled Liber *Algorizmi de Numero Indoren.* The importance of this publication in the development of European sciences is well-recognized. Adelard translated al-Khwarezmi's another work under the title of *Liber Ysogogarum.* Thus Central Asia was instrumental in the introduction of the decimal system and the concept of zero of Indian origin to the Europe.

Abu Mashar al-Balkhi was highly influenced by Aryabhatta's *Ardha Ratrika* in his study of astronomy. Some Uighur texts found in Turfan deal with lunar calculations based on Indian astronomy. The famous Bower manuscripts found in Central Asia deal with Indian system of medicine. Abu Mansur Muwafaq appreciated and adopted Indian system of medicine. Hamara Pal came to India, learnt *ilmi tibb,* returned to Transoxiana and practiced medicine as *tabib hakim* and *jarrah.* Abdurrazzaq Samarkandi had appreciation for Indian drugs and brought some of them for use in Central Asia.

Scholars have noticed similarities in the paintings in India and Central Asia. The unique blending of Indo-Turani style in miniature painting was noticed at the turn of the sixteenth century. The Mughal miniature painting, to a great extent, owes to Central Asian masters for its evolution. Some Central Asian miniaturists of seventeenth century followed Indian style of miniature painting, especially those of the Delhi masters. Many miniature painters and calligraphers came from Central Asia and served in Mughal courts. Farukh Begh, a Qalmaq, joined Akbar's service. Muhammad Nadir Samarqandi and Muhammad Murad also came from Central Asia.

There were various sources through which Indian handicrafts, artisans, mechanics, stone masons and builders found their way into Central Asia. Timur brought large number of them to Samarkand. Horticulturists from Iran and Turan helped in the cultivation of trees. Skilled hands from Turkistan and Persia, under the patronage of Akbar, sowed melon and planted vines.

Indo-Central Asian contact was not restricted to the medieval period only. The links exist from the ancient period. Again the flow of men, materials and the ideas was never unidirectional. It was a two-way process. Shakas, Hunas and the Kushanas migrated to India in historic period. Shakadwipi or Maga Brāhmīns of Central Asian origin have prominent place in Indian society. Indian epics, *Purāṇas, Jatakas,* Jain texts, fables, etc. have numerous mentions and descriptions of the places, persons, mountains, rivers, etc. of Central Asia. Shakas, according to Indian tradition, belonged to India and were of *Kshatriya Varna.* They might have migrated to the Central Asian region in remote past. The same is the case of the Yavanas or the Ionian Greeks.

The Urdu language owes its origin to the Indo-Central Asian contact during the medieval period. 'Urdu' itself is a Persianized Turkish word, which originally meant 'the camp of a Turkish army'. In India, it means 'court' or 'camp'. The language, in its initial stages, was known as 'Hindi' or 'language of Hind or India'. It was also known as 'Hindwi' or 'Hindostani'. This language travelled to different places of India with Sufis or Muslim mystics, freely accepted various regional or local influences, and as also known as Gujari, Dakhni or Dehlavi.[84] Hindi language was also influenced by Turkic language. The number of Turkic words in Hindi, according to Dr. Bhola Nath Tiwari, a noted scholar, is not less than 125. Some of the Turkic words in use in Hindi language are: Urdu, Bahadur, Uzbak, Turk, Chaku (knife), Kainchi (scissors), Qabu (in control), Chammach (spoon), Top (cannon), Topachi (gunner), Barud (gun-powder), Biwi (wife), Chechak (small-pox), Lash (dead body), Sarai (inn) and Bewarchi (cook). Suffix chi of Turkic language is very much in use in Hindi.[85]

India's commercial and cultural contacts with Central Asia extend to pre-historic times. India's trade with China in one hand and Europe on the other and its cultural intercourse with them partly depended on the Silk Roads through the heart of Central Asia. Central Asia and the Indian community living there played vital role in the trade relations between India and Russia. N.B. Baikova in her monograph (*Rol' Srednei Azii V Russko-Indiiskikh Torgovykh Svyazakh;* Role of Central Asia in Russo-Indian Trade Relations; Tashkent, 1964) has shown that the Central Asia was the connecting link in the trade between the two countries between first half of the sixteenth century to the second half of the eighteenth century. Publication of another volume provides further information in this direction. It was published in 1965. The documents published in Moscow in 1958 throwing light on

Russo-Indian relations and the ample work done by Russian and Central Asian scholars provide ample material for study in this field.[86]

A colony of Indian sattlers existed in Astrakhan since 1630s. Bukhara also emerged as the chief point of concentration of the Indians. Spread over all Iran, Afghanistan, Uzbekistan, parts of Central Asia and India, they were a great help in transmission of money through letters of credit.[87] Pyotr Pashino, a Russian orientalist traveller and journalist, who visited India twice, reported about the Indians in Central Asia during early 1870s. He collected the materials by personally talking to Indians residing in Tashkent. He also used the materials collected by others from Bukhara and other places of Turkistan. According to him, the natives of Delhi, Bombay and other cities of India lived in many places of Central Asia.[88]

Indians occupied several caravan sarais in Tashkent, Bukhara and Samarkand; had homes close to one another in old Margelan, which were known as Indian rows. Nemangan city also had Indian quarters.[89] It may be mentioned that the Central Asians living in India had also their separate quarters or Mahallas, such as the Mahalla-i-Khwarezm Shahi, Mahalla-i-Samarqandi, Mahalla-i-Khitai, Mahalla-i-Atabegi. A separate mahalla in Ahmedabad was named after Bukhara. Haji Sadr Shah of Bukhara settled two villages—Shadrpur and Shahpur, which continue to exist as Shahpur and Shakarpur.[90] Such colonies existed in Central Asia, at least, since seventeenth century and in India since the time of Akbar and Jehangir. Many Indians were merchants trading in items traditionally exported from India. But there were skilful jewellers, bookbinders, weavers, bakers, and farmers also among them. The merchants acquired monopoly position in the tea trade in Bukhara; they opened tea packing enterprises in Samarkand. They sold indigo, muslin, cotton fabric, rugs kimonos, dyes, iron, copper and steel pots, sugar, etc. They exported raw silk, Russian porcelain discs and manufactured goods from Central Asia to Afghanistan, Kashgar and India.[91]

The relation of the Indians with locals was cordial. They maintained friendly relation with the people of the cities and the villages of the region. The merchants maintained good relation with their Central Asian counterparts. Indians were also the source of information about India and its culture for the people of Central Asia. Indian traders established contacts with Central Russian firms after the region became part of Russia.[92]

Babar was the founder of his own empire in India. He came from Farghana valley. He has written much about his native place, about the wars he fought in his native place, in his *Babarnama.* He compares and contrasts, gives massive information about the land, the climate, and the people, their way of living, housing, village settlement pattern, vegetation, fruits, etc. He detests India's heat and dust; nostalgically remembers Central Asian melons. Abul Fazl mentions about the cultivation of melons in India. Not only *Babarnama* and *Ain-e-Akbari,* but the memoirs of others of Delhi Sultanate and Mughal kings also provide information about Central Asia, the Sufis and others coming from there.

Many travellers from India have written their accounts of the land and the people of Central Asia. M.N. Roy, Raja Mahendra Pratap, Rahul Sankrityayan and others visited the region and have written about the same. Raja Ranjit Singh of Punjab sent his envoys there. Mohan Lal wrote his travel accounts. Iqitidar Sidiqi was there. *Tarikhe Munajile Bukhara* by Fazil Khan is a well-written book. Unlike Britishers, who had the tendency to denigrade, the Indian travellers wrote about the region and the people with warmth and as they saw it.

In Hindi language, the History of Central Asia by Rahul Sankrityayan is published in two volumes *(Madhya Asia kā Itihās). Sārthavāh* (in Hindi) by Dr. Motichandra provides valuable information about the trade routes between India and Central Asia. However, much more need to be done by Indian and Central Asian scholars to rediscover their links from the ancient days to the present. The works of some of the scholars in this case needs mention, which are: *The Geography of the Purāṇas* by S.M. Ali, Cunningham's *Ancient Geography of India,* edited by S. Majumdar Sastri, N.L. Dey's *The Geographical Dictionary of Ancient and Medieval India* and D.C. Sirkar's *Cosmography and Geography in Early Indian Literature.*

Problems of Proper Interpretation

Icons and paintings of many excavations are not properly interpreted due to various reasons. Eminent Indologist, Dr. Lokesh Chandra has pointed towards misinterpretations of certain icons of Central Asian origin. A head from Khocho with the third eye of Śiva and all the features of that divinity was interpreted as that of a *devata.* Fragment of a wall-painting, found in the rubble of temple number 9 at Bezeklik was identified as the head of a Brahmana. In reality, it is that of the Nilakantha Avalokiteshvara appearing as the metamorphosis of Śiva, the great Yogin, in the *Nilakantha-sutra.* Fragment of a mural painting from the Second Domed Cave, Kumtura is that of Vasishtha and Arundhati, and not, as broadly identified, of a Brāhmīn. The silk painting of an 'Angry Arhat' found by the Third German Expedition at the lower end of the cave of Eighty-four Siddhas on the foothills near Turfan, is, in reality, that of Dingnāga. Professor Lokesh Chandra has properly explained Tukhara melody and Tiered Stupa with niches in proper historical perspective.[93]

Central Asian Role in Spread of Buddhism and Indian Culture

Central Asia played crucial role in the spread of Buddhism and the Indian culture. A large number of earliest Buddhist missionaries in China (Loyang) belonged to western Central Asia. Among them, there were two Parthians (An Shih-kao and An Hsuan), three Tusharas or Yueh-Chih (Chi Lou-chia-chi'en or Lokakshema, Chih Vao and Chin Liang), two Soghdians (K'ang Meng-hsiang and K'ang Chu). K'ang Chu came from K'ang-chu, which is known as 'Kangyu' in Russian literature and 'Kank' in Indian classical literature. Among the translators of Buddhist literature in Chinese, before the end of western Chin dynasty, 6 or 7 were Chinese, six were Indians and sixteen belonged to Central Asian communities. Of the last category, there were six Yueh-chis, four Parthians, three Soghdians, two Kucheans and one Khotanese.[94]

An Shih-kao (his Chinese name) was a Parthian crown prince, who abdicated his throne in favour of his uncle; dedicated his life for religious work; went to the East; settled in Loyang in 148 A.D. and translated up to 170 texts. Many men whose ancestors migrated from western Turkistan engaged themselves for the spread of Buddhism.[95] Parthian scholar associated with the school of translators of Buddhist texts in China, apart from Ngan-She-Kao or Lokottama, was Ngan-Hivan. Kasyapa Matanga and Dharmatrata founded the school, but Ngan-She-Kao made the first organized effort in this direction. Indo Scythian monk Lokakshema was also among the first group of translators. Senghui, a Sogdian was the first to introduce Buddhism in southern China. Scores of Central Asian scholars like Kumarajiva contributed immensely towards the dissemination of Buddhist religion and thought in Central Asia and

China through expositions and translations of sacred texts. Some of the best specimens of the Central Asian Buddhist scholars were Buddhabhadra, Sanghabhuti, Gautam Sanghdeva and Punyatrat.[96] Apart from the Parthians, Sogdians, Indo-Scythians, Kucheans and Khotanese, the other teachers of Buddhism in Central Asia were Uighurs, Tibetans and Mongols. Central Asia has produced many Buddhist savants. It had also the Buddhas and Boddhisattvas; Amitabha, Avalokita, Manjushri and Kshitigarbha had Central Asian and Chinese linkages.[97] Sylvain Levi suggests that Manjushri was of Tokharian origin. Indian tradition links him with China. According to I-tsing, he dwells in China. Lokashema was also of Tokhara origin. Ghoshak was an important Buddhist scholar who was born in Tokharistan. A point which needs mention in Central Asian context is that the scholarship there was not only confined to the Buddhist scriptures. Kumarjiva also studied four *Vedas*, five sciences, Brahmanical Shastras and astronomy at Kashgar,[98] during his return journey from Kashmir after his study of Buddhist scriptures. Like India, Central Asia had great centres of learning. Sarvastivadins popularized the study of Sanskrit. The people of different ethnicity speaking different languages lived harmoniously in Central Asia.

Place like Kucha in Central Asia was the centre of Indian influenced music from where it spread to China. Musical instruments were taken to China from Kucha. One of the teachers of lute in China was a Brāhmīn. Another lute-player, Sujiva was from the Royal house of Kucha.[99]

Buddhism was dominant; it was in flourishing state. Yarkand and Khotan were the centres of Mahayana Buddhism. Kashgar, Kucha, Turfan and Shan Shan near Lob-nor were Hinayanist centres. The contact of the states of Tarim valley mentioned above was intimate and regular with India and the Oxus valley.

A very positive aspect of the culture of Central Asia was the harmonious co-existence of different religious groups and sects. There were Hinayanists in Mahayanist centres and *vice versa.* Brāhmīnism existed with Buddhism. Manichaeism, and Nestorian Christianity also were practiced by some.

Language and Literature: Links and Interactions

As discussed earlier, Urdu language owes its origin to the Indo-Central Asian contact. Hindi has large number of Turkic, Persian and Arabic words. Other Indian languages also have the words from these languages. Persian was the official language during the Mughal rule in India. Russian scholars have discovered some Indic languages in Central Asia. Pariah of Hissar Valley speak an Indic language of the same name in their homes. They communicate in Uzbek and Tajik languages with their neighbours.[100]

Central Asia is a polyglot society. Different languages were spoken in Tarim and Oxus valleys. Linguistic scene did not remain the same at all the time. The language scenario changed with the change in the ethnic composition with passage of time. Two languages were spoken in the early centuries of the Christian era, in Xinjiang. The northern language was named Kuchean It was also called Tokharian or the language of the Tokharas or Indo-Scythians. The language, with two great western and eastern groups, was supposed to be an Indo-European language. The language spoken in southern Tarim basin was called 'Saka' and 'Khotanese'. The three other languages, written in the script of Aramaic origin, were Iranian languages. Two of them have preserved Manichean texts. Sogdian, the language of the region around Samarkand contained Buddhist, Manichaean and Christian texts.[101]

Uighur, literary form of the various Turkish idioms spoken north and south of Tien Shan, derived its name from the Uighur script, derived from the Syriac. It was widely used for Buddhist, Manichaean and Christian literature. Its use for Buddhist literature increased when Uighurs replaced Tibetan power in Tarim valley in about 860 A.D. and founded their own kingdom. Tibetan manuscripts have also been found in Khotan, Miran and Tun-huang regions. Prakrit recension of *Dharmapada,* and other documents known as Kharosthi documents have been excavated from Xinjiang. The language (Gandhari Prakrit) and the script (Kharosthi) of the same are Indian. Wide use of Sanskrit in Central Asia, especially by the Sarvastivadin Buddhists, is a well known fact. Khotanese, Agnean, Kuchean, Sogdian, Uighur, Turkish, Monghol, Manchu and Chinese manuscripts or tracts or the fragments have been recovered from Central Asia.[102]

Presently, Turkic languages are spoken in Uzbekistan, Kazakhstan, Turkmenistan and Kirghijistan. Tajik spoken in Tajikistan is an Iranian language. Uighur is a Turkic language. Some religious minorities speak their own languages.

Apart from the scripts mentioned above, Brahmi was widely used in Central Asia. Its introduction in Central Asia and association with Buddhism is supposed to be of earlier date than that of

Kharosthi. Three varieties of this script are traced in Sanskrit texts found there. The script was also used for writing Agnean (language of Agnidesha), Kuchean and Saka-Khotanese.[103]

The discoveries of an inscription of the first century B.C. in Tazikistan and an inscription on gold slab found at Dalverzin in Uzbekistan and some other inscriptions at Wardak and Kunduz in Afghanistan take us back before the Christian era, so far the use of Prakrit is concerned. As mentioned earlier, Kharosthi documents were discovered from various archaeological sites in the Tarim basin, in Khotan, Niya, Endere, Miran, Lou-lan and Kurak Darya. Over two hundred documents written in black ink in Kharoshthi script on different materials — wood, leather, silk and paper—were discovered. Sir Aurel Stein wrote: "At the Niya site, I found by the hundred wooden documents comprising correspondence, mainly official, contracts, accounts, miscellaneous memoranda and the like, all written in that Sanskrit language and the Kharosthi script which during the first centuries before and after Christ were used on the Indian north-west frontier and in the adjacent portions of Afghanistan."[104] The inscriptions received at Miran were fresh even after the lapse of two thousand years. A large number of coins struck in Khotan or nearby places were also in the same script. The coins dated first century B.C. to first century A.D.[105]

Sanskrit was methodically taught in Central Asia. It was called 'Arshi' (Arya) in Tokharian. Many Sanskrit manuscripts, like that of Ashvaghosha's *Buddha Charit* and *Saundarānand Kavya* (discovered from Shorchuq), were found out in Central Asia during various excavations. Almost all the important Buddhist texts were translated in all the major Central Asian languages. The scholars not only studied the texts and translated them, but also wrote commentary on the texts. Grammar, astronomy and all other subjects were methodically taught and studied. Bower manuscripts discovered at Kucha are medical texts.

The languages of India and Central Asia had profound impact on each other. Genesis and development of Urdu and Turkic lexemes in Hindi are the results of Indian and Central Asian contact. Sanskrit has also the profound impact on the languages of Central Asia. The language of the region also had impact on Sanskrit. The Shaka and Slav languages, which were spoken in Central Asia, were intimately linked with Sanskrit. The relation of Turkic languages with the Aryan languages is very ancient.[106]

Caldwell has given voluminous data and massive analysis of the links of the Turk-Mongol languages with South Indian language in general, in his *A Comparative Grammar of the Dravidian of South Indian Family of Language.* The work, however, had many shortcomings. Caldwell links Dravidian languages with the Sythian languages of Central Asia. However, the Scythian is a very loose grouping and therefore, his study lacks sharp focus.

Some valuable information is also available in the *History of Central Asia* written by Rahul Sankrityayan in Hindi language. The vocabulary of Russian language given by him shows massive lexical similarity with Sanskrit. Here, it needs mention that the difference between the languages of *Rigveda* and *Avesta,* and that between Sanskrit and old Persian is mostly phonetic, and not grammatical. The Iranian languages of Central Asia and Iran are intimately related to the Indo-Aryan languages.

Dr. Ram Villash Sharma, a well-known Indian scholar, has brought many lexical, phonetic, morphological and syntactical similarities of Turkic and Mongol language with Indian languages in his Hindi publication, *Bhārat ke Prāchīn Bhāshā Parivār aur Hindi.* Dr. Sharma compares the languages of Turk-Mongol and Fino-Ugrian family with the languages of India. He compares phonetic, lexical, morphological traits of Turkic, Mongol (Khalkh, Buriat) and Fin languages with those of the Indian languages. Turkic, like many Indo-Aryan and Dravidian languages shows the tendency of palatization.

The syntactic pattern of Indian languages, except Khasi and Kashmiri is 'Subject-object-verb'. Turkic language also follows the same. However, like in Sanskrit in "gachchhami' (I go; gachchh, to go); in Turkic 'galirim' (I come); the pronominal suffix follows the verb. Neither Sanskrit 'ami' or 'mi', nor Turkic 'im' are freely used as first person singular pronoun, I, as is done in Bengali and Marathi. The word for 'I' in these languages is 'aham' and 'ban' respectively. Turkic language uses pronominal suffix after the noun as in 'babam' (my father; baba = father, -m = my). It needs mention that 'Baba' is also used for father in many Indian languages. The pattern of adding pronominal suffix as well the suffix for 'I' in this case is of Indian origin. Arabic and Persian also follow the same. Both Hindi and Turkic add the verb denoting 'to do' to the noun to make verb ('karana' in Hindi, 'kam karna, to do the work; 'kilmak' in Turkic, namaj kilmak, to do or perform namaj). In many cases, new meaning comes when two words are added and density of meaning is achieved by reduplication of words. The pattern of the formation of higher numerals in Turkic, Dravidian and many Munda and Indo-Mongoloid languages is the same.[107]

New discoveries in Central Asia and India during colonial days have brought out huge material about the culture and languages of the two regions. However, the colonial studies has also the drawbacks. In many cases, the cultural and linguistic continuum, both in terms of time and geographical spread was ignored; differences, rather than the similarities were emphasized.

The facts are often explained with narrow focus and mis-interpreted. It needs mention that Indo-Central Asian linkages operated on wider canvas. The areas from Central Asia through India to South-East Asia and from West to East Asia shared many cultural traits. The precepts of divine kingship, apotheosis/deification of kings, cult syncretism, composite cult emblems, law, bureaucratic government and expressions in arts, norms, values and the ethos conformed in a large area from Central Asia to South East Asia. Deification of Kushana kings, the kings of Java and Cambodia and that of India treated as Viṣṇu's incarnation are not isolated phenomena. The writings of the Nicolo Seals of Central Asia (*Miarark, Yasnu, Oezo*; meaning *Mihir*; Vedic God *Mitra* or Sun, Viṣṇu and *Isa* or *Śiva*) pointed towards the same phenomenon as we find in '*Surys-Sevana,* (worship of sun god; in reality the Sun and Śiva are identified and worshipped together) in Indonesia and *Panchayatan Puja* (worship of five gods together) in India.[108] Kharosthi documents found in Central Asia show the similarity in the social and cultural fields with India. The similarities extended to South-East Asia also. India, Iran, Greece, Central Asia and South-East Asia, in reality, formed a vast culture zone during Classical period. There existed cultural continuum in the areas mentioned above and the study of the cultures and languages in 'continuum frame' may remove haziness of ideas and may bring clarity in our perceptions.

Reconciliation and amalgamation of myths and local adaptations operated in Central Asia also. It is believed that Asanga, a well-known Buddhist scholar, effected the amalgamation. Rhys Davids has confirmed the same.[109]

The study of the history and culture of the people with colonial past, at a time, suffers due to Euro-centric bias of the scholars.

The Indian scholars mostly rely on the translations of their classical literature by the foreigners. Their outreach to the original Russian, Central Asian, Chinese and Tibetan sources is poor. The work by Indian and Central Asian scholars may bring new facts to light and remove perceptional haziness. It is necessary that Indian and Central Asian scholars undertake massive study of each other's languages, society and culture. The gap in our knowledge about each other is a real one and needs to be bridged.

References

1. Mansura Haider, 'India and Central Asia: Linkages and Interactions', *in Central Asia, The Great Game Replayed,* An Indian Perspective, Edited by Professor Nirmala Joshi, Delhi, 2003, p. 257.
2. *Ibid.*
3. S. P. Gupta, 'Pre-historic Indian Culture in Soviet Central Asia', in *India's Contribution to World Thought and Culture,* pp. 239-48.
4. Mansura Haider, *op. cit.*, p. 264.
5. Pentti Aalto, 'On the role of Central Asia in the Spread of Indian Cultural Influence', in '*India's Contribution.....*', p. 249.
6. *Ibid.*
7. *Ibid.*
8. B.N. Puri, *Buddhism in Central Asia,* Reprint, Delhi (2000), p. 332.
9. *Ibid.*, p. 271.
10. Chhaya Bhattacharya, 'India — A Major Source of Central Asian Art, in '*India's Contribution...*', p. 292.
11. *Ibid,* pp. 294-95.
12. *Ibid,* p. 297.
13. Mansura Haider, *op. cit.*, pp. 273-74.
14. *Ibid,* pp. 271-72.
15. S.P. Gupta, *op. cit.*
16. R.H. Sulamanov, *Indian Parallels in Ancient Cults of Sogdiana,* The paper presented in a Seminar on "India and Central Asia (Pre-Islamic Period)", in Tashkent (2000), Mimeographed.
17. S.P. Gupta, 'Hindu Gods in Western Central Asia: A Lesser Known Chapter of Indian History; *Dialogue,* Vol. 3, No. 2; April-June 2002, Delhi, pp. 142-43.
18. *Ibid.*, p. 143.
19. Yuriy Burayakov, 'The Issue of Relation between Sogd and Indian in the *ancient times and the early middle ages*; paper presented in 'India and Central Asia (Pre-Islamic period) seminar held in Tashkent in 2000.
20. P. Banerjee, Hindu Deities in Central Asia, in '*India's Contribution to the World Thought and Culture,* pp. 281-87.

21. Dunitriyen, G.L.; 'From the History of Indian Colony in Central Asia, in *Indian and Central Asia: Cultural, Poltiical and Economic Links* by Surendra Gopal, Calcutta (2001), p. 82.
22. *The Cultural Heritage of India,* Calcutta (1991), (heritage referred as 'Heritage...') vol. VI, pp. 221-23.
23. *Ibid.*, p. 223.
24. *Ibid.*, p.223-24.
25. Panini, *Ashtadhyayi,* V. 4. 74; VI. 3. 97.
26. *Cultural Heritage of India,* Vol. VI. p. 8.
27. S.M. Ali, *The Geography of the Purāṇas,* New Delhi, 1996, p. 37.
28. *Ibid.*
29. *Cultural Heritage of India,* VI, p. 11.
30. *Ibid.* quoted from *Mahabharata,* VI. 5. 12.
31. *Ibid. Mahabharata,* VI. 6. 4-5.
32. *Ibid.*, VI.6. 8, 13, 37-38.
33. *Ibid., Markandaya Purāṇa,* LIV. 12ff.
34. *Matsya Purāṇa,* CXIII. 26.31.
35. *Markandaya Purāṇa,* LV. 20ff.
36. *Brahmanda Purāṇa,* XXXV. 50.
37. *Shri Viṣṇu Purāṇa,* 2. 2. 34-38
38. Ali, S.M.; *The Geography of the Purāṇas,* New Delhi, 1996; p. 87.
39. *Ibid.*, H. Raychaudhari, *Studies in Indian Antiquities,* (Calcutta, 1932), pp. 75-76.
40. Raychaudhuri, *op. cit.*, p. 75.
41. Ali, *op. cit.*, p. 97.
42. N.L. Dev, *The Geography Dictionary of Ancient and Mediaeval India,* London, 1927, p. 74.; quoted in *The Cultural Heritage,* p. 12.
43. Kumar, B.B.; Central Asia: The Indian Links; *Dialogue,* 3:4, April-June 2002, Delhi; p. 175.
44. Valmiki's *Ramayana; Kiskindha Kand,* 43.39-59.
45. *Ibid.*, 43. 12
46. *Ibid.*, 43. 55. 60.
47. *Mahabharata,* Sabha Parva, 53. 17.
48. *Ibid.*, Bhishma Parva, 6.1.31; 7.2.
49. *Ibid.*, Adi Parva, 17.
50. *Ibid.*, Sabha., 52. 13-17.
51. *Ibid.*, Udyog Parva, 4.15.
52. *Ibid.*, Sabha, 28. 11-15.
53. *Ibid.*, 52. 13-17.
54. *Ibid.* 52.6.
55. *Ibid.*, 51.23-24, 30.
56. *Ibid.*, 78.60.
57. *Ibid.*, Bhishma Parva, 75.21.
58. *Ibid.*, Karna Parva, 77. 19.

59. *Ibid., Harsha Charit* 760; *Kavya Mimamsa,* Last part of Chapter III; *Mahabharata* XIII. 836.
60. *Vāyu Purāṇa* 4.7.44; *Matsya Purāṇa,* 121. 45-46.
61. Kumar, *op. cit.*, p. 176.
62. Kumar, B.B., *Looking East,* Dialogue 5:1, July-September 2003, p. 7.
63. *Cultural Heritage of India,* Vol. II, pp. 614-16.
64. *Shrimad Bhāgvata Purāṇa,* 9.8.4-7; *Shri Viṣṇu Purāṇa* 4.3.42-48.
65. *Mahabharata.*, Anu., 33.21-23.
66. *Ibid.*, 33.21; *Kovel Jataka,* 6, p. 110.
67. *Mahabharata,* Anuśāsan Parva, 35. 17-18.
68. *Manu Smriti,* X. 43-44.
69. Agnihotri, Dr. Prabhu Dayal, *Patanjali-Kalin Bharat* (Hindi), pp. 92-93.
70. Penti Aalto, Helsinki, The Name of Tashkent.
71. *Ibid.*,
72. *Mahabharata.*, 2.47.1850.
73. *Mahabharata.*, 12.65.2429.
74. *Shrimad Bhāgawat Purāṇa,* 2.4.18.
75. *Ibid,* 9.20.30)
76. Communicated by Professor Lokesh Chandra during personal communication.
77. Meenakshi Jain, 'Secularism: The Indian Historical Experience;' Dialogue, Vol. 5, No.1; October-December 2003; New Delhi; p. 47.
78. *Ibid.*
79. Mansura Haider, 'India and Central Asia: Linkages and Interactions;' in Nirmala Joshi's *Central Asia,* p. 261.
80. *Ibid.*, p. 258.
81. *Ibid.*, p. 259.
82. *Ibid.*,
83. Mansura Haider, *op. cit.*
84. *The Cultural Heritage of India,* Vol. V, pp. 642-43.
85. Bhola Nath Tiwari, *Hindi Bhasha,* p. 183. (hereafter Tiwari).
86. Dr. Surendra Gopal, *India and Central Asia, Cultural, Economic and Political Links,* Delhi (2001), pp. VII-VIII.
87. *Ibid.*, pp.26-27.
88. A. Lubarasky, 'Indian Settlers in Central Asia', Chennai, *Vivekanand Kendra Patrika,* Vol. 2, No. 1, February 1973, p. 108.
89. *Ibid.*
90. Mansura Haider, *op. cit.*, pp. 267-68.
91. Lubarasky, *op. cit.*
92. *Ibid.*, pp. 108-09.
93. Lokesh Chandra, 'Notes on Central Asian Buddhist Iconography', *Dialogue,* Vol. 3, No. 4, pp. 33-42.
94. B.A. Litvinsky, 'India and Soviet Central Asia', in *India's Contribution,* p. 268.

95. B.N. Puri, *Buddhism in Central Asia,* pp. 322-23.
96. *Ibid.*, p. 172.
97. *Ibid.*, p. 141-43.
98. *Ibid.*, p. 325.
99. B.N. Puri, *op. cit.*, pp. 242-43.
100. I.M. Oranskii, 'An Essay on the Ethnography of a group of Indic Language Speaking Pariah (in the Hissar Valley)' in *India and Central Asia* by Surendra Gopal; pp. 139-42.
101. Tiwari, pp. 179-81.
102. *Ibid.*, pp. 182-84.
103. *Ibid.*, p. 186-87.
104. Aurel Stein, *Ancient Central Asian Tracts,* Masṭillan & Co., London, 1955, p. 28.
105. Samarendra Nath Sen, 'India and the Ancient World; Transmission of Scientific Ideas', *in Cultural Heritage,* Vol. VI, p. 228-29,
106. Ram Vilash Sharma, *Bharat ke Prachin Bhasha Parivar aur Hindi,* Vol. 2, Delhi, (1983), p. 243.
107. *Ibid.*
108. B.B. Kumar, 'Looking East', *Dialogue,* Vol. 5, No. 1, p. 8.
109. P. Banerjee, *op. cit.*, pp. 282-83.

2

Land and People of Central Asia in Ancient Indian Literature

References of the land and the people of Central Asia abound in ancient Indian classical literature. Apart from the *Vedas, Pūraṇas,* epics and *Manuśmṛti,* we find their mention, at least, in Kalidasa's *Raghuvaṁśa,* Kalhana's *Rajataraṅgini,* Kṣemendra's *Bṛhata Kathā Mañjari,* Somdeva's *Kathā Sarit Sāgara,* Rajaśekhara's *Kāvyamīmāṁsā* and Visākha Dutta's *Mudrā-Rākṣasa.*

Central Asia in Vedic Literature

The Indian Classical literature categorizes Central Asia under *Udichya* or *Uttarāpatha* (Northern Region). There is mention of *Aupamanyava Kamboja's* teacher, Sage *Madrakar Shaungāyani* in the *Vaṁśa Brāhmaṇa* of Sāma Veda.[1] As the very name indicates, they belonged to the Kamboja (Hindukush and Pamir) and its close neighbourhood, Madra. Similarly, Uttara Madras and Kambojas were close neighbours.[2] Again, there are regions, such as, *Param Kamboja, Uttar Madra* and *Uttar Kuru,* which were definitely located across the Himalayas in Central Asia. *Bāhlika Uttara Madras,* as mentioned in *Aitareya Brāhmaṇa,* clearly refers to the Madras settled in Bactria (*Balkh; Bāhlika*). *Aitareya Brāhmaṇa* also refers about Uttara Kuru and Uttara Madra.[3] *Atharva Veda* takes the names of many Central Asian communities together at one place. They are Shakas, Yavanas, Tuṣāras and Bāhlikas (*Śaka, Yavana, Tuṣāra, Bāhlikāshcha*) in Uttarapath. Their juxtaposition, as elsewhere the juxtaposition of other tribes, indicates them to be neighbouring tribes. It also makes reference to Gāndhāri, Mujāvat and Bāhlik from the north-west. These are Gandhāras, Mujāvat (land of *Soma;* Kamboja region or Hindukush-Pamir regions) and Bactrians respectively. *Atharvaveda Parisiṣṭa* juxtaposes the Kambojas, Bāhlikas and Gandhāras at one place.[4] It also makes the first direct reference of Kambojas.[5]

The contact between India and Central Asia takes us to the remotest past. The inhabitants of Uttar Kuru seem to be legendary fellows in the epics and later literature, but as historic ones in *Aitareya Brāhmaṇa,* according to the author of *Vedic Index.* Uttar Kuru is the divine land (region of *Devas,* i.e. gods) for Vasiṣṭha Satya Havya, but Atyārāti wants to conquer it.[6] Indians remember *Jambudvipa,* which includes Central Asia, in *Sankalpa* part of their prayer almost everyday.[7]

Central Asian Geography in the *Purāṇas/Bhuvan-kosh* and Epics

Geography of the known world, known as *Bhuvan-kosh,* and history is the essential part of every *Purāṇa.* According to the *Purāṇas,* the earth consists of seven *dvipas.* Ordinarily, the term '*dvipa*' means island. Panini derives it as *dvi* + *āp,* meaning 'land between two arms of water'.[8] But the Puranic *dvipas* stand for continents or tribal or national territories.[9] It signified 'all types of natural or human regions – big or small'.[10] The barriers may be water, sand, swamp, high mountains or thick forests.[11] Jambudvipa is at the centre of all seven *dvipas* of the world. Mount Meru is at the centre of the Jambudvipa. It needs mention that 'Mount Meru' is the Pamir knot; India and Central Asia are parts of the same, according to the geography of the *Pūraṇas.* It needs further mention that some scholars tried to identify specific geographical regions basing on the details of the mountains, rivers, vegetation, climate, etc. of the dvipas given in the *Pūraṇas.* Al-Beruni, as for example, located Pushkardvipa between China and Mangala (perhaps, China and Mongolia).[12]

Jambudvipa, also known as the Sudarśandvipa, is said to be circular in shape[13] and surrounded by the sea in all the sides. It has six mountain ranges – Himālaya, Hemakūta, Nisadha, Nila, Sveta and Shringāvat.[14] – and nine zones (*varshas*) – Hari, Bhadrāśva, Ketumāl, Bhārata, Uttar Kuru, Sweta, Hiranyaka, Airāvata and Ilāvṛta.[15] Jambudvipa is depressed in the south and north; it is

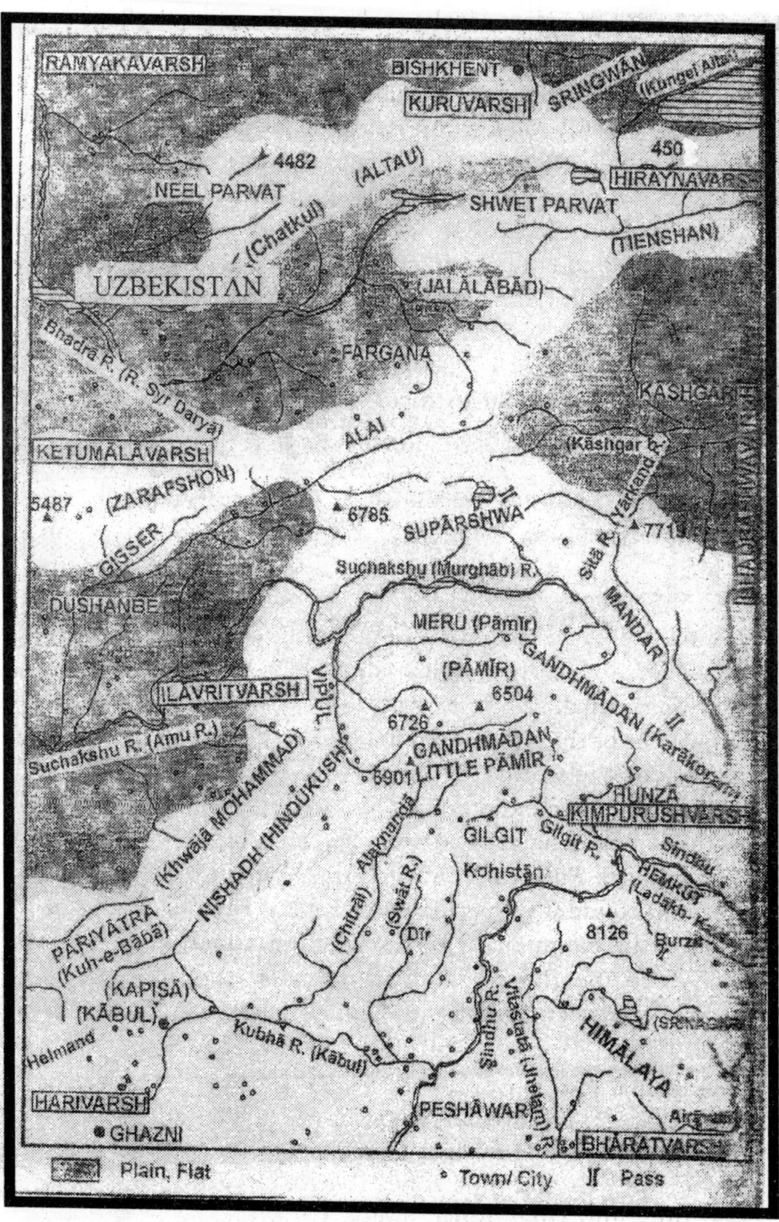

Mountains and Regions of Jambu Dvipa

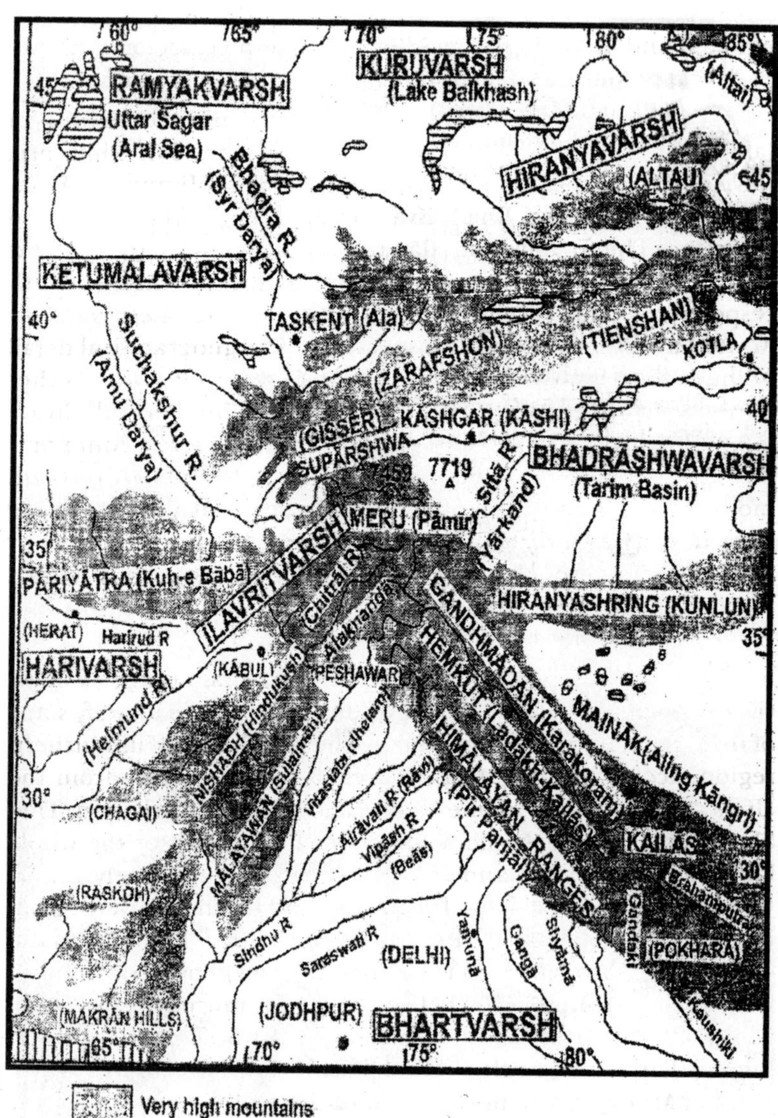

Geography of Jambu Dvipa

elevated and broad in the middle.[16] The elevated region is known as Ilāvṛta or Meruvarṣa; Mount Meru is located in its centre.

According to the *Purāṇas*, there are nine divisions of Jambudvipa. According to *Matsya Purāṇa*, the nine divisions are: Ilāvṛta, Ramyaka or Ramanaka, Hiranmaya or Hiranyaka, Uttar Kuru or Shriṅgaśaka, Bhadrāśva, Ketumāl, Hari, Kimpuruṣa and Bhārata.[17] The first division, Ilāvṛta, is centrally located. The next three and the last three are located in the north and south respectively. The remaining two, Bhadrāśva and Ketumāla are located in the east and west respectively. The geographical detail of the regions is given in the *Mahābhārata, Bhiṣma Parva* and other *Purāṇas*, e.g. *Mārkāṇḍeya Pūrāṇa*[18] and *Brahmāṇḍ Purāṇa*[19] divide Jambudvipa into four regions like four petals of a lotus. Four rivers flow from Mount Meru, namely Sitā flowing to the east through mountains to the Bhadrāśva region to the sea; Alakanandā flowing towards the south through India to the sea; Chakṣu (or Vakṣu or Oxus) flowing through the mountains towards west to the Ketumāl region, and Bhadrā flowing through northern mountains and Uttar Kuru region to the sea.[20]

Vāyu Purāṇa details the geography – mountain ranges, valleys, river systems, etc. of Jambudvipa making it possible to identify some of their geographical features today. The description of its northern region, according to S.M. Ali, 'covers a very vast area—from the Urals and the Caspian to the Yenisei and from the Turkestan, Tien Shan ranges to the Arctic. It describes topography of the whole land very accurately and in some cases picturesquely ......'[21] Bhadrāśva, in the east, is the Tārim basin and Hwāngho river region, i.e., the whole of Sinkiāng and Northern China'.[22] Ketumāl, to the west of Meru through which river Chakṣu (Oxus) flows, corresponds to western Turkestan.[23] It is believed to cover 'practically the whole of the ancient Bactria which included the whole of the present Afghan Turkistan (north of Hindukush), the Harirude valley, the basin of Murkhab system (all south of the old bed of Amu Darya) and basins of the Surkhan, Kafirnigan, Vakhsh and Yaksu rivers...'.[24] Hari[25] and Bhārata represented western Tibet and India respectively. The area around Meru, the mountainous region, was Meruvarṣa or Ilāvṛta. The area across Himalayas and Hindukush from Pamir up to arctic was known as Uttar Kuru. Arctic was known as Somagiri.[26]

Central Asia in the Epics

There is numerous mentions of the Uttar Kuru and Somagiri in the Vālmikī's *Rāmāyaṇa* and *Mahābhārata,* the two epics. There is graphic picture of the region in Vālmikī's *Rāmāyaṇa.*[27] While sending the monkeys to the north for searching Śitā, Sugriva describes the land routes and the countries in that direction. Among others, he commands them to search Śitā in the lands and towns of the Dardas, Kambojas, Yavanas and Shakas.[28] He describes Uttar Kuru and Somagiri (the arctic region): 'There is the sea and the Somagiri in the extreme north. The route is extremely difficult one. The region is without the sun, and yet very much lighted. There are no national boundaries there.[29] As described in the *Mahābhārata,* Arjuna brought water from the northern sea for the coronation of Yudhiṣṭhira.[30] There is description of the Meru (Pamir), Meruvarṣa around it, Bhadrashwa to its east, and Uttar Kuru to its north.[31] The conference of the Devas (gods) was held at Mount Meru to decide about the churning of the sea.[32]

Central Asian People in the Classical Indian Literature

The different communities of Central Asia were not only known to the Indians in remote past, but were even the part of the Indian social system. *Mahābhārata* asserts that Central Asian communities — Śaka, Darada, Pahlava, Kirāta and Pārada — are said to be Kshatriyas of good birth.[33] Manusmṛti also says the same, according to which, Śakas and Yavanas were degraded Kshatriyas reduced to the status of Vrishalas (*Vṛṣala*).[34] In this case, it is relevant to bring Sagara legend, detailed in the *Mahābhārata* and *Purāṇas,* to notice. As we know, Sagara was an ancestor of Rama, born 24 generations earlier.[35] Sagara's father, Bāhu (Asita) was wrongfully defeated by the combination of Haihaya and Tālajangha Kshatriyas, in association of Śakas, Yavanas, Kambojas, Pāradas and Pahlavas; he was evicted from his kingdom, went to the forest and lived in the *ashrama* of a *rishi,* where Sagara was born. Sagara, on attaining adulthood and after coming to know of the injustice done to his family, took revenge on his father's enemies. He defeated and killed Haihayas and Tāljanghas in war, and wanted to kill their supporters also. Vashiṣṭa, Sagara's *Guru,* however, persuaded him to spare others. But, as advised by Vashiṣṭa, they were forced to abandon their religiously ordained duty, and thereby declared dead while living (*Jivanamṛta*, the men; abandoning the ordained duties, were declared dead while living). Śakas, Yavanas, Kambojas, Paradas and Pahlavas became *Vṛṣala* (*Vrātya*, degraded Kshatriya, Kshatriya Shudras).[36] In this context, it needs to be pointed out that the Sagara legend indicates towards two possibilities: (i) that political, linguistic, cultural and religious boundaries of India extended far beyond the Himalayas, Pamir and Hindukush, and (ii) there was outward migration of Central and West Asian communities from India. In reality, Patanjali, in his *Mahābhāṣya*, considers Śakas and Yavanas to be the migrants from India.[37] Here, it needs mention that *Mahābhārata* points towards the downwards social mobility of tribes, mentioned above, several times. It says that Śaka, Yavana, Kamboja and Mahashaka Kshatriyas became *vṛṣala* due to not availing the benefits of the contact of the Brāhmaṇas;[38] Tusharas and others were degraded due to lack of proper conduct;[39] some other Kshatriya communities were also degraded due to their envy for the Brāhmaṇas.[40]

Participation of Central Asian communities in *Mahābhārata* war, and their participation in the *Rajasūya yajña* of Yudhiṣṭhira find numerous mentions in the *Mahābhārata*. Panchāla king, Drupada, the father of Draupadi and father-in-law of Pāndavas, asks Yudhiṣṭhira to invite Central Asians — Śakas, Pahlavas, Riṣik and Darad kings — to participate in the *Mahābharata* war from Pandava side.[41] Of course, Yudhiṣṭhira was late in doing so. Sudakṣina of the Kambojas with one *akṣauhini* army of Kamboja, Śaka and Yavana army fought the war from Kaurava side.[42] Sudakṣina was appointed one of the ten army Generals by Duryodhana.[43] Tuṣāra (Yueh-chi of the Chinese; Kuṣanas of Kaniṣka's community) also fought the war from Kaurava side.[44] They were ferocious warriors.[45] Tuṣāras were also present in the Rājasūya *yajña* of Yudhiṣṭhira.[46] As mentioned in the *Mahābhārata*, Arjuna brought tribute from Uttar Kuru.[47] and another Pandava hero Nakula defeated Huṇas, Pahlavas, Yavanas and Śakas.[48] Yudhiṣṭhira received tribute from Uttar Kuru.[49] Shakas, Huṇas and Tuṣāras paid tribute to Yudhiṣṭhira.[50] The name of Tuṣāra-Giri (Tushara Mountain) finds mention in *Mahābhārata*, *Harṣcharita* and *Kāvyamimāṁsā*.[51] The fact that Chakṣu river (Oxus or Amu Darya) flowed through Tuṣāra,

Lampaka, Pahlava, Parada and Śaka countries, according to *Vayu* and *Matsya Purāṇas,* indicated the geographical location of these communities.[52]

Kaṅka is the name of the Sogdians, i.e. the people of Samarkand. The name comes with the names of other Central Asian communities in *Mahābhārata.* At one place, it comes with Śakas and Tuṣāras (*Śakas Tuśārāḥ Kaṅkāsch*);[53] yet at another place with Śakas, Tuṣaras and Pahlavas (*Śakas Tuśārāh Kaṅkāsch Pahlavāshch*).[54] Kaṅkas are mentioned twice in Bhāgwat Purāṇa, together with Kirātas, Huṇas, Yavanas, Khasas and others,[55] then again with Kirātas, Huṇas, Khasas, Śakas and others.[56] In *Mahābhārata,* usually the contiguous tribes are clubbed together, except when social factors are concerned.

The inhabitants of the region around Samarkand were known as Sogdians. In *Mahābhārata,* the people are mentioned as Cūlikas along with Tuṣāras, Yavanas, and Śakas, occupying the right flank of the army in the war.[57] Culikas or Cūlikas are also mentioned along with the tribes inhabiting the northern borders of India, such as, Lampākas, Kirātas, Kāśmiras, etc. according to *Mārkandeya Purāṇa.*[58] Cūlikas, as mentioned in the *Matsya Purāṇa,* founded a kingdom in a corner of India during *Kaliyuga* (dark age).[59] It also mentions their names along with the Aparāntikas, Pañcadakas, Tārakṣuras and some other tribes.[60] *Brahma Purāṇa* names Śūlika, and *Brahmāṇḍa Purāṇa* Jhillika; the other readings of different manuscripts give Culikam, Vulika, Vumika, Vutika and Vrulika. Among various usages, mentioned, Culika, Cūlika, Cūika, Śūlika Śūlika and Sulika, the most frequently used names are the Culika and the Sulika. Sulikas, like Culikas, mentioned in the company of Tukhāras, Yavanas, Pahlavas, Cinās, etc., live in the country watered by Cakṣu river (Vakṣu; Oxus). Their location, according to Matsya Purāṇa is in the North, whereas, according to Brihatsamhitā (Bṛhatsaṁhitā), mentioned six times therein, places them towards the North-West.[61] The community also finds mention in other books, such as Charak Saṁhitā and various lexicons.[62] In Charak, the name comes along with the names of Bāhlika, Pahlika, Pahlava, Cina, Yavana and Śaka.[63]

In a Sanskrit-Chinese vocabulary (Fan-yu-tsa-ming of Liyen) and in another fragmentary lexicon, the equivalent of Suri (= Suli) is given as 'Hu' (barbarian; the term applied by the Chinese only to the Sogdians during that period). It is mentioned in the company of *Pārasi* (Pārasika), *Truṣaka gaṇa* (Turuṣka), *Karpiśaya* (Kapiśā), Tukhāra *Kucinaṁ* (Kuchā), etc. The Tibetans and Pahlavās called them Sulika (also Śulik) and Pahlavās Surāk (pronounced as Sūlik). From all the facts mentioned above, it is clear that variation in the nomenclature in Indian literature is due to carelessness of the copiers and also due to phonetic changes, as the interchange between s, ś and ch is commonly observed in Middle Indo-Aryan, even in India. Thus, the Sogdian name Śulik and Śūlik may be phonetically changed to Culik and Cūlik. Therefore, the Chulika identity (with Sulika and Sūlika as its variants) with Sogdian is quite evident. The Cūlikā-Paiśāci Prakrit (Chūlikā Paiśāchī), as discussed elsewhere, as the language of the Sogdians, seems to be a variety of the Prakrit spoken in North-West India.

The Sogdians, as is well-known, were traders with colonies everywhere in Central Asia, and also in China. They even migrated to India; there identity with Chalukya dynasty, Solanki Rajputs and some communities in Punjab is reasonably suggested. This phenomenon should be viewed in the context not only of cultural and linguistic continuum, but that of the ethnic continuum also between India and Central Asia.

In *Ramayaṇa* of Valmiki, the mythical origin of Kambojas, Yavanas, Shakas, Paradas and *Mlechchhas* through the divine power of Rishi Vasishtha's *Kāmadhenu* is given.[64] It also mentions about the import of horses from Kamboj and Bāhlika (Bactria) by the princes of Ayodhya.[65]

As discussed above, considerable information about the land and the people of Central Asia is available in the classical Indian literature. *Kāvyamimāṁsā* of Rajsekhara, Kalhan's *Rājataraṅgiṇi*, some lexicons, Sanskrit and Buddhist prose narratives and fables, etc. provide valuable information. Guṇādhya's *Brihatkathā*, Somdeva's *Kathā-saritsāgar*, Kshemendra's *Brihat-Kathā-Mañjari* and its Jain adaptation, *Vasudeva-Hiṇḍi*, Kalidasa's epics and dramas, especially, *Meghdoot* and *Vikramorvashiam* provide enough insight about India's neighbourhood — Himalayas and Uttar Kuru.[66]

Rajashekhara, in his *Kavyamimaṁsā*, provides an exhaustive list of Central Asian communities, which include Śakas, Tuṣāras, Vokanas, Huṇās, Kambojas, Vāhlicas, Pahlavas, Tanganas, Limpakas, Turuṣkas, etc.[67]

King Lalitāditya Muktapīḍa of Kashmir, as mentioned in *Rājataraṅgiṇi* of Kalhaṇa, undertook a war expedition against his northern and north-western neighbours — Kambojas,Tusharas, Daradas, Strirajya, Uttar Kuru, etc.[68] He also humiliated the Huṇas in war.[69]

Kshemendra[70] and Somadeva,[71] in their works mention above, detail the successful war efforts of King Vikramāditya against the hordes attacking India from across the northern mountains.

Kalidasa furnishes graphic picture of India's northern mountains, the Himàlayas, and Uttar Kuru in his *Meghdoota, Vikramorvashiaṁ* and *Raghuvaṁśa. Raghuvaṁśa* details the war efforts of King Raghu against the Pārasikas (Persians), Huṇas and the Kambojas of Uttarāpath (Northern Region).[72]

Visākh Dutta's Buddhist drama *Mudrārākṣas* describes Chandragupta's alliance with Himalayan king 'Parvatak' against Śakas, Yavanas, Kambojas, Kirātas, Parasikas and Bāhlikas.[73]

According to *Sutrālaṅkar,* a painter of Pushkalāvati visited the country called *Ashmaka,* meaning stone or stony, and out of his piety decorated a Buddhist monastery. The country was identified with Tashkent. Incidentally, it needs mention that there is a tradition that *Sutrālaṅkar* was written by Ashvaghosha. Others attribute its authorship to Kumārlāt. Here it needs mention that the word *Tāsh* in Tashkent is linked up with stone. Its old name is *Chăch*; Pulleyblank wanted to connect it with Yenisseian word for 'stone'; Ket. t*yes,* Kot. s*hish,* Pumpokolsk *cys.* He sees it as a relic of Huna occupation of the Sogdiana in the fifth or sixth centuries. However, as the word finds mention in the inscriptions of Shapur I (240-272 A.D.), it had earlier currency. In the old Chinese records, Tashkent is transcribed with the hieroglyph 'shish' that is stone. The name linked with Turkic *tash,* 'stone' may be a translation of the earlier older names. The old ,name *Chach* also had the meaning 'stone'. The inhabitants of the area, according to the Chinese sources', were *Chiang chu* or *K'ang chu.* It may, very likely, be of Tukharian origin. *K'ang* may mean some kind of stone in Tokharian. In Hindi *kankar* is pebble. In Indian classical literature, as discussed earlier, *Kanka* is the word for Sogdians and *Aṣmak* for Tashkent.[74] The syllable *kent* or *kand* in Tashkent, Samarkand, Yarkand seems to be the same as the Sanskrit word *kanthā.* This word has come in

Aṣṭādhyāyī of Paṇini. The word in *Kashikā Sūtra* denoted 'town' or 'city'. Tashkent and Yarkand, I am told, were also known as *Dākshikanthā* and *Yahvarkanthā* respectively. The Sanskrit term for 'Turk' is '*Turuṣka*'. The first syllable of the name is found in the name of 'Turvasu' in Classical Indian literature. The second syllable *ṣka* is a superlative suffix found in the name of Kaniṣka; the meaning of 'Kaniṣka' is the 'youngest son'.[75]

The last syllable of numerous country and place names in Central Asia is *stān* (Sanskrit *sthān*; Persian *stān*). Some old geographical names have changed; some other names are still used with slight variation. River 'Sitā' of Chinese Turkistan is Tarim river today; Khotamn and Kustan is Khotan; Gandhār, Kubhā, Gomati and Vakshu have changed to Kandahar, Kabul, Gomal and Oxus respectively. Names, such as Shaka, Kushan and Huna continue to remain in use. Such examples may be multiplied. Kashyapa (Kaśyapa) was a seer and progenitor of the living world, according to Indian mythology; Bhrigu (Bhṛgu) was a seer. The 'Caspian Sea' and 'Phrigia' (called Phrugia by the Greeks) reminds us of the names of 'Kashyapa' and 'Bhrigu' respectively. We should examine whether *phoenic* in *phoenician* is not related to Sanskrit *Baṇic* (the trader).[76]

References

1. *Vamsa Brahmana,* 1:18.
2. Law, Dr. B.C.; *Vedic Index,* 138; *Some Kshatriya Tribes of Ancient India,* 1924; pp. 230-31.
3. *Aitareya Brāhmaṇa,* VIII.14.
4. *Atharva Veda—Pariśiṣta* 57.2.5.
5. *Ibid.*
6. *Mahabharata, Karṇa Parva,* 77.19; *Harsha Charit* 760; *Kavya Mimāṁsa,* last part of Chapter III; *Mahābhārata* XIII.836.
7. *Vāyu Purāṇa* 4.7.44; *Matsya Purāṇa* 121.45-46.
8. Panini, *Asṭadhyāyi,* V.4.74; VI, 3.97.
9. *Cultural Heritage of India,* Vol. VI, p. 8.
10. Ali, S.M., *The Geography of the Purāṇas,* New Delhi, 1996, p. 37.
11. *Ibid.*
12. *Cultural Heritage of India,* VI, p. 11.
13. *Ibid.,* quoted from *Mahābhārata,* VI.5.12.
14. *Ibid., Mahābhārata,* VI.6.4-5.

15. *Ibid.*, VI.6.8.13; 37-38.
16. *Ibid., Mārkandaya Purāṇa,* I.IV, 12ff.
17. *Matsya Purāṇa,* CXIII.26.31.
18. *Mārkandaya Purāṇa,* I.V.20ff.
19. *Brahmānd Purāṇa,* XXXV.50.
20. *Shri Viṣṇu Purāṇa,* 2.2.34-38.
21. Ali, S.M., *op. cit.*, p. 87.
22. *Ibid.*, H. Raychaudhari, *Studies in Indian Antiquities,* Calcutta, 1932, pp.75-76.
23. Raychaudhari, *op. cit.*, p. 75.
24. Ali, *op. cit.*, p. 97.
25. Dev, N.L., *The Geography Dictionary of Ancient and Medieval India,* London, 1927, p. 74; quoted in the *Cultural Heritage of India,* p. 12.
26. Kumar, B.B., 'Central Asia: The Indian Links; *Dialogue,* 3;4, p. 175.
27. Valmiki, *Rāmāyaṇa, Kiṣkindha Kanḍ,* 43.39-59.
28. *Ibid.*, 43.12.
29. *Ibid.*, 43.55-60.
30. *Mahābhārata, Sabhā Parva,* 6.1.31; 7.2.
31. *Ibid., Bhishma Parva,* 6.1.31; 7.2.
32. *Ibid., Adi Parva,* ch. 17.
33. *Ibid.*, Sabhā, 52.13-17.
34. *Manusmṛti,* X.43-44.
35. Saroj Bala, India: Scientific Dating of Ancient Events from 7000 B.C. to 2000 B.C. – Covering Rigvedic and *Ramayana* Eras; *Dialogue,* Vol. 15, No. 1; p. 122.
36. *Shrimad Bhāgvaṭa Purāṇa* 9.8.4-7; *Shri Viṣṇu Purāṇa* 4.3.42-48.
37. Agnihotri, Dr. Prabhu Dayal, *Patañjali-Kālin Bhārat* (Hindi), pp. 92-93.
38. MB, Anu., 33.21-23.
39. *Ibid.*, 33.21; Kovel Jatak 6, p.110.
40. *Ibid.*, 35.17-18.
41. *Ibid., Udyog Parva,* 4.15.
42. *Ibid.*, 5.19.21-22
43. *Ibid.*, 5.155.30-33
44. *Ibid., Bhiṣma Parva,* 75.21.
45. *Ibid., Karṇa Parva,* 77.19.
46. *Ibid., Sabhā Parva,* 78.60.
47. *Ibid.*,28.11-15.
48. *Ibid.*, 52.13-17.
49. *Ibid.*, 52.6.
50. *Ibid.*, 51.23-24, 30.
51. *Ibid., Harsh Chariṭ* 760; *Kavya Mimāṁsa,* last of chapter III; *Mahābhārata* XIII.836.

52. *Vayu Purāṇa* 4.7.44; *Matsya Purāṇa* 121.45-46.
53. *MB* 2.47.1850.
54. *Ibid.*, 12.65.2429.
55. *Shrimad Bhāgwat Purāṇa* 2.4.18.
56. *Ibid.*, 9.20.30.
57. *Mahābhārat,* VI.75.3297.
58. *Mārkaṇḍaya Purāṇa,* 57.40.
59. *Matsya Purāṇa,* 50.76.
60. *Ibid.*, 58.37.
61. Bagchi, *India and Central Asia* ; pp. 142-43.
62. *Brihatsaṁhitā,* IX, 15, 21; X.7; XIV.23; XVI.8; Śaulika in XVI.8.
63. Vālmīki, *Rāmāyaṇa,* Bāl Kānḍ, 1.55.2-3.
64. Charak Saṁhita, 20.8.
65. *Ibid,* 1.6.22.
66. Kumar, B.B, *India and Central Asia: Links and Interactions* in Roy, J.N. & Kumar, B.B. (Ed.), *India and Central Asia: Classical to Contemporary Periods*; New Delhi, 2007; p. 14.
67. Rajashekhara, *Kavyamimāṁsa,* Ed. Gaekwad's *Oriental Series,* I (1916, Chapter 17; Introduction, p. XXVI).
68. Kalhana, *Rajatarangini,* 4.164-174.
69. *Ibid.*, 4.178-80.
70. Kshemendra, *Bṛhat-Kathā,* 10.1.285-86.
71. Somadeva, *Kathā-Saritsāgara,* 18.1.76-78.
72. Kalidasa, *Raghuvaṁśa,* 4.66-70.
73. Visakh Dutta, *Mudrārakṣas,* 2.
74. Kumar, B.B., *op. cit.*, p. 15.
75. Information based on personal communication from Dr. Lokesh Chandra.
76. Kumar, B.B., *op. cit.*, p. 16.

3

Central Asia : The Land and the People

There is hardly any anonymity about the areas covered under Central Asia, as the term is not properly defined. Geographically, Central Asia has two parts, namely 'Eastern Central Asia' and 'Western Central Asia'. Whereas the Western Central Asia includes Kazakhstan, Kyrghyz Republic, Tajikistan, Uzbekistan and Turkmenistan, the eastern region includes Tibet and Xinjiang. Some people include even Mongolia in Central Asia; whereas others label it as 'Inner Asia'. In the Soviet usage, only the four southern Central Asian Soviet republics and southern part of Kazakhstan was included in Central Asia. Geographically, Central Asia is divided into northern steppes from South Russia to Manchuria, inhabited by the nomadic people, and the southern zone, inhabited by sedentary people. The latter zone included oases of the Tarim basin, usually known as Xinjiang or Eastern Turkistan.

Saka Tribes and the Land of their Habitation

The northern part of western Central Asia, consisting of Kazakhstan and northern part of Kyrghyz Republic, also known as *Uttarāpath* (northern route) and 'thirsty land', used to be nomadic; whereas southern part, *Dakṣināpath*, the region south of Aral sea and Syr Darya consisting of Uzbekistan, Tajikistan and Turkmenistan used to have much settled population. Uttarapath has the vast desert. The region of seven rivers (*Saptanad, Semi-rechye*) between Talas and Ili rivers, although small part of Uttarapath, used to be most densely populated region of immense historical and cultural importance. Tien Shan and Altai mountain ranges are located on its south-eastern and eastern ends respectively. The Illi River breaks the continuity of the Tien Shan and Altai mountain ranges. The region has two important lakes of Issyk kul and Balkash. Altai was always famous for its gold and copper mines, and a source of the import of gold for India and other Asian countries. The word 'Altai' itself means gold in Turk and Mongol languages. Huns disrupted the supply route of the same, which Greek-Bactrian king Euthudim (225-189 BC) wanted to open, but could not succeed. Daksinapath has the deserts of Kyzil kum and Kara kum, apart from fertile river valleys and oases.

Ethnically, the northern nomadic zone was divided into western region from South Russia to the valley of Ienessi River, inhabited by the nomadic hordes of Aryan stock, called Scythians, and eastern region, including Outer and Inner Mongolia, Manchuria and further east, inhabited by Turco-Mongol hordes. The western region of the southern zone, between the Jaxartes or Syr Darya and Oxus, i.e. Amu Darya, was settled by people of Iranian stock. In the eastern region, from Pamir up to the frontier of China, lived Aryan-speaking people of different affiliations.[1]

As discussed elsewhere, there are numerous mentions of Central Asian communities in classical Indian literature. The accounts of Herodotus and the old Achamenian inscriptions provide earlier information about the nomadic Scythians. Indians called them Śaka and their area of inhabitation 'Śakadvipa'. They were called Śaka by the Persians, Skuthoi by the Greeks and Ashkuzai by the Assyrians. They were the nomadic sections of the Indo-Iranian people, speaking distinct dialects. According to the old Persian inscriptions, there were three nomadic Scythian tribes, namely (i) Saka Haumavarka, (ii) Saka Tigrakhauda, and (iii) Saka Taradraya. The first category was the Sakas mentioned in Indian and Persian literature, who were settled in region of Ferghana and extending upto Kashgar. The second category, the Sakas of 'pointed caps' occupied the valley of Jaxartes; they were spread towards the Aral. The third one lived beyond the sea up to the border of Russia. Herodotus mentions about other Scythian tribes also, such as Sarmatians, Massagetes, Arimaspes, Issedones, etc.[2] According to Rahul Sankrityayan, the term 'Sarmat', derived from *Sarvamāt* (Sanskrit, *sarva* = all; *māt*; matṛ, *mātā* = mother), was the name of the community because mother (women) had superior status in their society. As we know Saka women used to participate in war also.[3] The war between the Iranians and neighbouring Sakas, in which Iranians were defeated and their king Kurav was killed in 529 A.D., was led by the Saka queen, Tomuri.[4] Massagetes (*Massyagata* < *Matsyagata*; Sanskrit, *Matsya* = fish) were the fishermen living near Aral; they spoke an Iranian language. Arimaspes (Iranian, lover of horses; *asp*, Iranian< *aśva*, Sanskrit = horse) and Issedones lived towards the east in the northern steppes. The former, perhaps a Finno-Ugrian tribe, lived in the region of Irtych and Ienissei.[5]

Historically, the land between Danube in the west to Tien Shan-Altai mountain range belonged to the Sakas (Scythians), which Indians call *Śakadvipa* (Shakadvipa; Sakasthan, land of the Sakas; Sakastan, Seistan). During iron age (700 B.C.) dividing line between Sakas and Aryans, who were linguistically and culturally cousins, was from the north of the Aral Sea to the Syr Darya; Sakas lived to the north of the same and Aryans to the south. While Aryans were in Iron Age, the Sakas were yet in the Bronze Age. Sakas used gold enormously. The situation started changing since 174 B.C.; Sakas were forced to migrate from Eastern Śakadvipa towards the west due to depredation of the Hunas, who still lived in their old homeland during the reign of Greek-Bactrian Kings (225-189 B.C.). Likewise, Tukhāras (Chinese, Yueh-ches) also remained in their old region of Eastern Tarim basin near Kansu in the neighbourhood of China.

Greek, Persian and Chinese sources provide certain information about Masagit, Shakarauka, Dahai, Khas, Wusun and Yueh-chi Sakas. Masagit Sakas lived in the region east of Danube River through north of Caspian Sea in between Aral Sea and Syr Darya and in lower Amu Darya basin, i.e. Khwaresm. Dahai Shaka nomads inhabited south of them on the shores of Caspian Sea. Parthians, who gave a dynasty to Iranians, emerged from them. Shakarauka lived in east of Masagit and west of Semi-rechye (*Saptanad*, Sanskrit = seven rivers; *sapta* = seven, *nada* = river) up to Tarim River and Issyk kul lake in the region north of Syr Darya. As Saibang emerged from them, they are also called pre-Saibang. Shakarauka is supposed to mean Shaka-oka (Shakasthan; *oka*, Sanskrit, house). Many scholars believe that Shakarauka and Shaka Haumwark were the same people. The Soghdians lived in the south of their area between Syr and Amu daryas. The Shakaraukas moved from right bank of Syr Darya during the reign of Darius to the western hills of Khojand in second century B.C. The ancestors of Wusun (pre-Wusun) used to live in Altai mountain region. Yueh-chi, known as Tushara (Tuṣāra) in Sanskrit literature, lived in the oases to the immediate north and south of the Tien Shan mountain up to the western part of the Kansu of the China, near Hwang-ho River. Branches of the Tukharas, living in Kucha, Karasahr, Turfan and the surrounding areas up to the time of Uighur invasion in the eighth century were merged in them. The other branch of Sakas lived in the Eastern Turkistan in the oases of Khotan, Kashgar, Yarkand Niya, Lou-lan (Lobnor region) up to Tunhuang. Tarim basin was the original home of the Khasas from which they moved across Karakorum to Gilgit and Kashmir, and then up to Kumaon and western Nepal. The names of Kashgar, Khashagiri in Xinjiang, Kaskar in Gilgit-Chitral, Kash in Kashmir, Khas and Khasia caste from Kashmir to Nepal, and Khaskura, a second name of Nepali language, remind us of the Khasas, a distinct Shaka community.[6]

The region from Altai to Tien Shan up to Talas River originally belonged to the Wusuns. Huns gradually grabbed Ili and Chu river basins leaving only Tien Shan (Issyk kul) hill area to them. The Wusun king sent tribute to Chinese emperor in 436 A.D., which indicates the existence of the former, at least, up to that period in that region. Kangs (Kaṅk) were the western neighbours of the Wusuns; their frontiers met in Talas River basin. Many scholars identify Kangs with the Soghdians. Farghana valley was towards the west and south of the Wusuns.[7]

Hepthals or Ephthalites were considered to be Huns in India and Iran. They were, however, Shakas, rather than Huns. Being highly influenced by Huns, they may be called Hunish Sakas. But the name given to them is 'White Hun'; Historian Prokop calls them White Persian. Soviet excavators, under Professor Shishkin, have discovered the remains of their capital city in Baraksha near Bukhara. They found the paintings of a king in Indian dress in a hunting scene. This exhibited the influence of Indian culture on them. The same fact is revealed by Torman's construction of Sun temple in Gwalior. Hepthalites extended their rule in parts of India. The two Hepthal kings, Torman and Mihirkul are well-known in India. Their coins reveal that they were not Huns. Whereas the Huns were usually beardless, the pictures of the two kings show heavy beards. In Torman's coins, being the exact copies of the Gupta coins, there used to be king's head and his name in Gupta script, and on the other side the picture of the peacock. Mihirkul's coins depicted the king's image, either standing or on horse-back with the name and on reverse side the image of Hindu goddess Lakshmi (Lakṣmi).[8]

Huns, K'iangs and the Chinese

The Huns (Huṇ; Indian – Huṇa; Chinese – Hiung-nu) were in the habit of regularly attacking and plundering the Chinese territory. After the Great Wall of China was built in 214 B.C., the Huns were successfully prevented from going to the fertile plains of the Yellow River. Shortly after that, different Hun tribes of Mongolia united to form a powerful empire which lasted for about three and a half centuries (209 B.C. to 160 A.D.). Now they changed the direction of their attack towards Kansu to the eastern Sakadvipa, so that to enter China from the West.

In the Kukunor area, south of the Yueh che inhabited territory, now the Chinghai province of China, lived a very powerful people of nomadic habits, called K'iang, supposed to be the ancestors of the Tibetans. But, even they, according to Chinese Annals, seem to have certain affinities with the Aryan nomads, perhaps due to the contiguity of the Tukharas. K'iangs intruded deep into Chinese territory from the West from about the fourth to second centuries B.C.[9]

Hun Depredation and Migration of Sakas

Hun's depredation in *Shakadvipa* (land of the Sakas; started some time only after that. The Saka people whom the Huns attacked and defeated, and killed their king in Kansu region were the Tukharas; Chinese called them Ta Yueh-che. In reality, when the Huns defeated the Tukharas in 176 B.C. and ousted them from their original homeland, the latter were divided into two sections, named by the Chinese Ta Yueh che (Great Yueh che) and Siao Yueh-che (Small Yueh che). While Siao Yueh che (numerically smaller section) moved to the south and merged in the K'iang population, the Ta Yueh ches moved to the west.[10] A large section of them, however, were merged in the invading Huns, and later on in the Turk population. During centuries, they migrated towards the south and west and merged in the population of India, Iran and the Slavs. As Rahul Sankrityayan says the Russians were also the descendants of the Sakas.[11]

During their migration away from home, the Great Yueh che took the north-western route along the foot of [illegible] Altai towards the Ili region rather than Tarim basin routes, reached the territory of the Wu-suns, defeated them, and stayed with them till Wu-suns revolted against them and drove them away. Being ousted from the Ili region, Yueh ches moved towards the west, reached Fergana, the territory called Ta-yuan by the Chinese. Fergana, along with Tashkent and Kashgar, was occupied by the Sakas — the Saka Haumavarka of the Achamenian inscriptions, Sakai of the Greeks and Saka (Sanskrit-Śaka) of the Indian literature. Sakas, after the occupation of Transoxiana by the Tukharas, and being ousted, occupied Sogdiana, and then moving southwards destroyed Greek kingdom of Bactriana, which became Tokharistan after the conquest by the Tukharas; Chinese called it Ta-hia. While occupying Oxus valley, Tukharas further pushed Sakas towards North-West India.

Here, it needs mention that even Tukharas belonged to greater Saka family. Tukharas were ousted from Kansu in 176 B.C.; they occupied Transoxiana in about 160 B.C.; established them in Oxus valley, and in 128 B.C., they were already the master of a powerful empire, when Chinese envoy, Chang-Chien came to meet them in Bactria to seek their help in controlling the Huns (Sanskrit Huṇ) and to request them to come back to their homeland in Kansu. After stabilizing their power in Oxus valley, they conquered Kabul and parts of North-West India forming powerful Kushan Empire, lasting up to third century A.D.[12] The greatest king of the Kushan (Kusaṇa) dynasty was Kanishka (Kaniṣka), a powerful enthusiastic patron of Buddhism. Balkh (Bactria) and Purushapur (Puruṣapura; Peshawar) were the places from where the Kushan emperors ruled.

The continuance of Hun depredation resulted into conversion of Eastern Shakadvipa into Huna land in the fourth century A.D. The Saka tribes of the west – Gaths and Saramats — living to the west of Done River on the shore of Black Sea also moved away towards north and west. As a result of this movement, the linguistic and ethnic texture of Central Asia changed considerably; the Greek-Bactrian state and Greek states in North-West India were eliminated.[13]

Hephthalites Replacing the Tukhāras

The next to take the place of the Tukhāras in Central Asia, and later on to affect the political history of India, Afghanistan and Iran, were the Hephthalites. There is confusion about their racial identity. Bagchi, like many others, calls them Hephthalite Huns; he includes them among the Turko-Mongol tribes, which, as discussed above, they were not. According to Chinese records, their community name was derived from the name of their ruling clan, called Ye-t'a or Hephtha; Persian historians named them Hayathelite, and Indian texts as Huna. An unimportant tribe, owing allegiance to the Turkish nomadic tribe of Juan-Juan in the beginning of the fifth century, they started moving westward, conquering the entire steppe areas up to Aral, incorporating the valley of the Ili up to Balkhas, the Valley of the Issiq-kul, the steppes of Chu and Chao, and the valley of the Jaxartes up to Aral sea. Sogdiana and Tokharistan, and perhaps Balkh also, were under them by about 440 AD. They conquered Balkh; attacked Khorasan in 484 and killed King Peroz; defeated one of the last remnants of the Kusans, the Kidara Kusan king in Kabul. After their domination up to Gandhar (Gandhara), they gradually crossed Sindhu. Though defeated by the Guptas in mid-sixth century, Haphthalites ruled Punjab and Kashmir for two generations, and merged in Indian population. In 516, they sent their ambassador to China. At one time, after their entry into India, the so-called Hun (Haphthalite) empire included the entire steppe from the upper Yulduz (north of Karasahr) to the Aral, Sogdiana, Merv, Eastern Iran, Afghanistan and Punjab.[14]

Turks in Central Asia

Next to dominate Central Asia were the Turks, who gave the name, Turkistan, to the Central Asian region. Kazakh, Uzbek, Kyrghyz and Turkmen, giving names to Kazakhstan, Uzbekistan, Kyrghyz Republic and Turkmenistan respectively, are Turk communities. Uighurs of Autonomous Uighur State of Xinjiang are also Turks. Turks were a Hunish tribe.[15] There old name was Assena or Ashina. They were an early converts to Buddhism.[16] The name of the community in Sanskrit is Turuṣka; Chinese called them Tu-kiu or Turkut, meaning 'strong'. Descendants of Huns had wolf as their totem; they lived in Altai region as subjects of Juan-Juans up to the beginning of the sixth century. When Juan-Juans became weak due to civil war in 520 A.D. between its two chiefs — A-na-kwei and his uncle Po-lo-men — the former, though victorious, had to face subordination of his Turkish vassals, as he became weak due to internal conflict. A Turk tribe, called Kao-kiu — same as Tolos, the ancestors of Uigurs —, who were already in conflict with Juan-Juans revolted against the latter in 521 A.D., and were defeated. A second revolt in 546 was also suppressed with the help of the Turks (Tu-kius). There was parting of ways between Juan-Juan and Tu-kiu tribes, when the request of the Bumin, the chief of the latter community for a Juan-Juan princess in marriage was turned down. The complete alienation between the two, led Bumin to ally himself with Toba Turks (Si-wei) of North China, and jointly crush the Juan-Juans in 552. The remaining Juan-Juans took refuse in China leaving entire Mongolia for the Turks. Bumin declared himself as Qaghan; established his capital at Orkhon. But he died in the same year.[17]

After Bumin's death, his son, Mu-ban and younger brother, Istami (She-tie in Chinese records) divided the empire of Mongolia into two. Mubin, controlling the Turk hordes up to Hami in the west called Eastern Turks, took the Imperial title of Qaghan. Istami, with the possession of western parts of the region with Western Turks under him, assumed the title of Yabghu. His empire comprised Zungaria, the valley of Irtych, Imil, Yulduz basin, Illi region and the region of Chu and Talas. His summer capital was at Yulduz and the winter capital on the bank of the Issiqul in Talas valley. Istami formed alliance with Khusroes Anoshirvan, the Sassanian emperor of Iran; they jointly attacked and destroyed the Hephthalite kingdom of his neighbourhood in 565; remnants of the Hephthalites were forced to migrate to Europe. The newly acquired kingdom was divided; Istami got Sogdiana, and Khosroes got Bactriana. Istami annexed Bactriana also to his territory without much delay. Tardu, the son and successor of Istami (575-603), attacked Tokharestan, bringing its two capitals, Balkh and Kunduz under his possession in 597-98. Hiuan Tsang found the country under a Turkish *tegin,* and a Turkish prince residing at Kunduz, when he visited the country in 630. Tardu assumed the title of Qaghan in 582, ending the previous practice of allegiance to the Qaghan of the Eastern Turks. He then allayed with China and together attacked the Eastern Turks. Their Qaghan, Ishpare found himself being attacked by Tardu from the west and Chinese (Kitan) from the east. Taking advantage of the prevailing situation, Tang emperor destroyed the power of Eastern Turks; brought the Turk chiefs under Chinese domination. China, however, maintained good relation with the Western Turks. But the Western Turks could not remain united. In 630, the Qarluq tribe revolted against Qaghan, She-hu and assassinated him. As a result, the Western Turks were divided into Nu-se-pi in the West and South-West of Issykul and Tu-lu in the North-West. Chinese army posted at Hami attacked and defeated Tu-lu in 641; the khanate of Western Turk was destroyed.[18]

Central Asia was attacked from the South-East by the Tibetans and from the South-West by the Arabs in the last part of seventh century. Chinese power weakened and Tibetans occupied Tarim basin in 670, and their rule lasted for about a century. Arabs defeated Iran in 639; In 652, they defeated Khwarezm, and then Balkh. Tushade, last king of Bukhara, was forced to accept Arab suzerainty and Islam, ruled for another 30 years as their vassal; Turkhun, king of Sogdh, continued to fight, ultimately he fled.

In 665, there was a great uprising against the Chinese domination; two tribes – Turk Nu-se-pi and Tu-lu – revolted against them; Qaghan Qutlugh organized Eastern Turks, who rallied their power under him. He organized his people; consolidated administration with the help of Tonuqus, an able and witty politician trained in China. His campaign, against Chinese in 682, resulted in harassment and ouster of Chinese from everywhere in the ancient Turk possessions. Mo-ch'o (Bakchur), Qutlugh's brother, succeeded him, after his death in 691, who ruled under the title Qupagan Qaghan from 691 to 716, carried his brother's policy against Chinese. The Chinese were defeated everywhere; all Turk tribes, including the two mentioned above, were united and brought under control leading to the creation of Turkish Empire. Mo-ch'o's succession, however, was disputed after his death; his son was killed by Qutlugh's son, who set up his elder brother, Mo-ki-lien as Qaghan. Mo-ki-lien ruled as Bilga Qaghan from 716 to 734. The information given by P.C. Bagchi and Rahul Sankrityayan, in this case, is confusing. Rahul Sankrityayan lists Kutuluga Biga (756 A.D.) under Uigurs, yet mentions the name of his successor Moinchura (759-760) as the first Uighur Kagan. It seems, there is mixing of Turk and Yughur dynasties in Rahul Sankrityayan's account.[19] Of course, Rahul Sankrityayan also traces parallel history of Uigurs. According to that, Jigin was the first king of Yuighurs; second one was Bosat (Bodhisatva; 629 A.D.). Moinchura, the tenth king (756-760) replaced Turks in Eastern Turkistan by bringing end to Turk dynasty there.

Karluk Turks ruled to the area west of them from 739 to 940 A.D. Their area gradually came under the influence of Arabs and Islam. Arab rule (673-818) was effective in Western Turkistan in the regions of Khorezm, Balkh, Samarkand, etc., but real power shifted from Arab to Turk hands not only in Western Turkistan, but even the entire Islamic state came under the Turks. Here, it needs mention that there was a war between the Chinese troops under Hau Syan chi and the Arab troops under its commander Jiyad bin-Saleh on the bank of Talas river during the mid-eighth century A.D., in which Arabs won. After that China could not come to Western Central Asia; the Arab power also became weak and they could not cross Talas and lost the ground to Karluq Turks in western Central Asia. In Western Central Asia, the spread of Islam was due to the joint effort of the Arab power and the Sufis. Kutaib, who was Arab governor, played a role in the early days, about which Rahul Sankrityayan writes:

"Islam hardly ever produced as zealous a propagator of the Islamic faith as Kutaib. In everyone of his campaigns, he forcibly converted the people to Islam but some of them afterwards returned to their old faith. In one of his campaigns, he destroyed the temple of fire worship in Samarkand and built a mosque instead, where a prize of two dirhams was offered to anyone who would join the *namaz* prayer. He placed an Arab in every household to act as an informer, a preacher of Islam and to live as the son-in-law of the family. The English historian Ross writes of him: "His character was an epitome of the qualities which made Islam a terror to mankind and ultimately conspired to reduce it to impotence."[20]

In Tarim basin, Arab power had no role in this case. The effort of conversion to Islam was mainly individual. Moreover, it came late. The story of the conversion of Khotan to Islam is full of fantastic miracles and impossibilities, but the main facts, as Ellsworth Huntington asserts, are historically accurate.[21] He writes:

"As per a chronicle (*tezgireh*) written by a scribe of Yusup Khadir Khan Khazi, king of Kashgar in 1000 A.D., four Imams came with the other Mohammedan invaders to convert Khotan, but the Buddhist "infidels" of Khotan clung to their faith. Then the four Imams by power of prayer destroyed their city, then called Khal-khalimachin. After that twelve thousand people became Mohammedans; built new city of Khotan; seventeen thousands of the remaining pagan inhabitants came to Choka with their king, Nuktereshid-Chuktereshid and built a new city. Forty years after that, the Imams followed them, but were refused admission. However, a man of Choka, who had become a Muhammedan secretly, came out by stealth and led them to water supply of the city. The exact source of the same was, however, not evident, as the water flowed in an underground conduit. The Imams prayed for guidance; a tree sprouted at once, grew to maturity, flowered and produced a delicate red crab-apple fruit, peculiar to the terrace villages. Knowing that there was water as the tree could not grow without the same, they dug a hole, discovered the conduit, and put red crab-apple in the same, which ultimately closed the conduit. As the water source dried up, the inhabitants abandoned Choka and moved eastward through Sai-bagh and Nura to Imamla on the Ak-Sai River. This, however, did not satisfy the Imams, who pursued them further, but failed as the Buddhists located upstream polluted the water flowing below. The Imams then dispatched a pious subordinate, whose fervent prayer caused the diversion of Ak-Sai eastward into the Kara Su. The hosts of Nuktershid then attacked the Imams and other Muslims during prayer and killed all of them. Forty of the killed, however, came to life and returned to Kashgar, persuaded its king to send persons to settle nomad inhabited Imamla, Sai-bagh and Nura. Nuktershid and his people moved south-eastward to Polu, an important post on Kalmuck road from Yarkand to Cherchen. The Buddhist Pagans, however, were ultimately conquered by the Muslims."[22]

The miracles, as mentioned above, were chiefly the distorted explanation of the real facts. Huntington further writes:

"The miracles, such for instance as the diversion of the Ak-Sai, are chiefly distorted explanations of real facts. The dates are open to question, for a while the chronicle gives 1000 A.D. as the time when Nuktershid ruled, Bellew gives 1095 A.D. Apparently, Choka was a provincial town in a district inhabited by nomads, and rose to importance only during the brief space when it became the capital of the Buddhist kings, whom the Muhammedans expelled from Khotan about 1000 A.D. The abandonment of the town was traditionally a withdrawal of the people without fighting because their water supply failed. Of course, the water supply may have been diverted by an enemy, as is said to have been done in the case of the Ak-Sai; but that does not explain where the water went, or why a town was ever founded with so diminutive a water supply as that now available, unless the climate were different."[23]

Mo-ki-lien's rule was not free from conflict; the war was fought against Tokuz-Oguz, Toquz-Tatar, Uigur and other tribes; relation with China was peaceful. But, the war with Basmil tribe brought an end to Eastern Turkish Empire in 744. Basmils, however, could not establish their own rule. Rather, Uighurs founded their empire with the help of another Turkish tribe, Qarluk, who ruled from 744 to 840 A.D.; Kutlug Biga was the founder, who died in 744; Sankrityayan, anyway, gives his period as 756. Kirghiz Turks, coming down from the region of Ienessei, captured Uigur capital Qarabalgasun and ousted the Uigurs from Mongolia in 840. Ousted from Mongolia, they settled in Qara-Khodjo (Khocho), ancient Turfan, Dzimsa, Qarasahr and Kucha in 843. Dzima became the Turkish Beshbaligh after their arrival. Their kingdom of Beshbaligh-Kucha lasted up to thirteenth century.[24]

Southern Central Asia

Khotan, the most important outpost on southern Silk Route, was perhaps the oldest one in Southern Central Asia. It was established at the time of Ashoka (Aśoka) with the blinded prince Kunal (Kuṇala) as its ruler. Southern part of Central Asia played most important part in the history of the cultural exchange between Indo-Iranian world and China. Bagchi writes: "The civilization of Chinese Turkistan up to about Tenth century was also mainly derived from India and Iran. This is why this region has been called by some scholars 'Indo-European oases'. The late Sir Aurel Stein, that indefatigable explorer of Central Asian regions, preferred the name Ser-India which the ancient Greeks had used. The use of this name has greatest justification for the simple reason that both China and India played a dominant role in shaping the civilization of this area." It was an area inhabited by Aryan speaking Tukharas (Yueh-ches), Bahlikas, Pahlavas, Kangs (Sogdians), Wu-suns and various other Scythian communities living right up to Kansu. The people living in Kucha, Karasahr, Turfan, etc. in northern Tarim basin were merged among the Turks after the Uighur invasion in eighth century.[25] He further writes, pointing towards the Indian linkages: "Herodotus (III, 98ff) seems to speak of all this area as a part of India. He says that part of India towards the rising sun is all sand, and that the country towards the east is a desert by reason of the sand. The desert people, according to him, were nomads, ate raw flesh and had Scythian customs in regard to the disposal of their old men and women. India proper is distinguished by Herodotus as the country lying towards the south of Persia, bordering on Caspatyros (Kashmir) and Pactyica (Pakhta). The inhabitants, according to him, resembled the Bactrians and were never subject to Darius."[26] British historian Toynbee takes the relationship in deep antiquity when he says that "Sanskrit speaking races" who were "spread from Hungary to North-West fringes of China" dominated Central Asia "from eighteenth century B.C. to fourth century A.D.".[27]

Religion of the People

Buddhism was the dominant religion of all the communities along with Vedic and Zoroastrianism in pre-Islamic period. The worship of Vedic/Zoroastrian gods -- Sun (*Mitra,* Ṛg Veda, Sanskrit; *Mithra, Mihir,* Avesta, Iranian) and Fire God (*Agni,* RV – prevailed). It is not that Buddhism, and even the Sun and Fire worship, disappeared altogether after the arrival of Islam under the banner of Arabs. The process was slow due to resistance. The Qarakhanids were mainly responsible for converting Tarim basin to Islam despite opposition from Uighurs, who were great patrons of Buddhism.[28] It needs mention that Uighurs were Turks, and the name of that particular Turk tribe was Aguj; Arabs called them Takuj-Aguj (also 'Toguj oguj' means new Oguj). The term used for their chief used to be *Yavagu;* Khakan, Qaghan, Khagan, Khan or Kahan was the title used by both the Mongol and Turk chiefs. Here, it may be mentioned that both Turks and Mongols emerged from Huns.

Buddhism among the Turks

It was Abu'l-Rayhan Muhammad al-Biruni, born in Khorezm, a learned son of Central Asia, who perhaps the first time wrote about the history of Buddhism in Central and Western Asia. He wrote: "In former times Khorasan, Persia, Iraq, Mosul, the country up to the frontier of Syria, was Buddhistic, but then Zarathustra went forth from Adharbayjan and preached Magism in Balkh (Bakhtra). His doctrine came into favour with king Gushtasp, and his son Isfendiyad spread the new faith both in East and West, both by force and by treaties. He founded Fire temples throughout his whole empire, from frontiers of China to those of the Greek Empire. The succeeding kings made their religion (i.e. Zoroastrianism) the obligatory state religion of Persia and Iraq."[29] He further wrote: "They worshipped idols, their remnants may now be found in India China and among the Toghuzghuz; the inhabitants of Khorasan call them'shamanan', from the Sanskrit *sramana.* All their shrines are the '*viharas*' of their idols and the 'farkharas' can (still) be seen in the border district of Khorasan adjoining India.[30] But, Sachau, the translator of Al-Biruni's book on India, was of the view that the latter was really not conversant with the factual history of Buddhism.[31]

Fa-Hian and Hiuen-Tsang wrote about the flourishing condition of Buddhism in Eastern Central Asia during the fifth century A.D. A.M. Belenitsky, however, writes that the true history of Buddhism in Central Asia is yet to be fully recapitulated.[32] Vambery mentions of the traces of Buddhism in Transoxania. Quoting Narshakhi, he writes about the two fairs in Bukhara where huge quantity of dolls used to be sold even during the Islamic period. He writes: "the traces of Buddhism in Transoxania can be found at the time of the Mohammedan conquest; for when Arabs took Berkend, and plundered it, among many other idols, one peculiarly large golden idol attracted their attention, which had in place of eyes two valuable pearls, which were sent as present to Haddjadj. Nay, long after the spread of Islam, Buddhism lingered in the memory of the inhabitants of Central Asia. Narshakhi tells us that two great fairs of dolls or images were held yearly at Bukhara and that often at one of these fairs as much as fifty thousand dirhems worth of toys changed hands. This, the Arabic author observes, comes from the old practice that prevailed, in the times when the Bokhariots were idolaters, of purchasing their idols at these fairs."[33]

The manuscript finds in Central Asia include Buddhist texts in Uighur, which in reality is the literary Turkish. These Turkish texts were the translations of the Tokharian Buddhist texts. The Turkish manuscript finds include the translations of *Maitreyasamiti-nāṭaka, Suvarṇaprabhāsa-Sūtra, Jataka, Sūtra of Kalyanakara and Pāpaṁkara.* Some the documents are in Brāhmī.

The Uigurs were Buddhists. They prayed to the Chinese monarch to allow the construction of Buddhist temple in 1001 AD and again in 1011.[34] They had Buddhist name, such as Damo (*Dharma*, Sanskrit), Pegu/Bogu (*Bhaga* = God, deity; Sanskrit).[35]

Turk Kagan Mo-gi-lyan (Mogliyan) was named after prominent disciple of Lord Buddha. Bosat (Bodhisatva; 629 A.D.) was the second Uighur Khakan.[36] Thus even their Khans adopted Buddhist names, which is significant. Apart from Buddhism, Hindu cults, gods and goddesses also formed part of the Central Asian belief system.[37]

Buddhism, though it somehow survived in Turfan up to early

fifteenth century, it lost the ground in Tarim basin, and the role of sword in the same has not been insignificant. Puri writes:

"Buddhist priests seem to have been massacred, as indicated by vaults filled with skeletons still wearing fragments of the monastic robe. Buddhism was not extinguished by this event, but lingered on here longer than in other areas of the Tarim basin. Even in 1420, the people of Turfan were Buddhists and according to the Ming Annals, there were more Buddhist temples than dwelling houses in Huo-chou (or Kara-Khoja).[38]

Hiuen Tsang wrote that only one language was spoken in Saptanada (Semirechye) and Chu valley. But language scenario gradually altered; there was loss of Scythian identity. However, it is not true that there was complete displacement. Most of the Scythians stayed back, merging their identity with the Turks.

Mountain across Khorgosh in Zinziang (China)

References

1. Bagchi, Prabodh Chandra; *India and Central Asia,* Calcutta (1955); p. 1.
2. *Ibid,* pp. 1-2.
3. Rahul Sankrityayan; *Madhya Asia ka Itihas* (Hindi), Vol. I, pp. 66, 68.
4. *Ibid.*, pp. 150-51.
5. Bagchi, *op. cit.*, p. 2.
6. Shankrityayan, op. cit., pp. 73-74.
7. *Ibid.*, pp. 98-103.
8. *Ibid.*, pp. 216-222.
9. Bagchi, *op. cit.*, p. 7.
10. *Ibid.*,
11. Sankrityayan, *op. cit.*, pp. 210-11.
12. Bagchi, p. 8.
13. Sankrityayan, *op. cit.*, pp. 64-65.
14. Bagchi, *op. cit.*, pp. 9-10.
15. *Ibid.*, pp.10-11.
16. *Ibid.*, pp. 11-12.
17. *Ibid.*, pp. 12-13; Sankrityayan, *op cit.*, pp. 243.
18. Bagchi, p. 13.
19. *A Thousand Years of Tatars,* p. 365.
20. Sankrityayan; *History of Central Asia,* p. 146.
21. Huntington, Ellsworth, p.166.
22. *Ibid.*, pp. 165-66.
23. *Ibid.*, p. 166.
24. Sankrityayan, *Madhya Asia ka Itihas,* Vol. I, p. 111.
25. Bagchi, *op. cit.*, pp. 13-14, 6.
26. *Ibid.*, p. 7.
27. Quoted by Prof. Raghu Vira, *India and Asia; A Cultural Symphony,* New Delhi, 1978; pp. 17-18.
28. Lokesh Chandra, *Cultural Heritage of India,* Vol. V; pp. 718-19.
29. Sachau, E.C. (translated); *Alberuni's India,* Vol. I, London, 1888, p. 21; Abureikhan Biruni, India, *Ishraniye proisvedeniya,* Vol. II, Tashkent, 1963, pp. 66-67; quoted by B.A. Litvinsky. India and Soviet Central Asia, in *India's Contribution to World Thought and Culture,* p. 263; hereafter 'Litvinsky'.
30. Litvinsky, *op. cit.*, pp. 263, 272 note.
31. *Ibid.*
32. *Ibid.*
33. Vambery, *History of Bukhara,* p. 15.
34. Sankrityayan, *op. cit.*, p. 253.
35. *Ibid.*, p. 237.
36. *Ibid.*, p. 242.
37. Lokesh Chandra (Ed.) *India's Contribution of World Thought and Culture,* pp. 281-88.
38. Puri, *Buddhism in Central Asia,* p. 79.

4

Land Routes linking India, Central Asia, China and the West

There were many land routes linking India and Central Asia. The land route linkages of India to China and the West were through Central Asia. China was also linked *via* North-Eastern Indian land route as well as through sea route. West had also direct linkages. Indian traders, at the close of 1880s, started bringing goods to Central Asia through Persia. This new trade route was less dangerous as well as cheaper. They asked for and received permission from the Russian authorities to use even a more advantageous route to Central Asia after the construction of the trans-Caspian Railways. The route was from Bombay port to Black Sea port of Batumi and then across Caucasus to Central Asia.[1]

The ancient land routes between India and Central Asia passed through the North-Western India, as well as through Kashmir. In North-Western India, Takshashila (Takṣaśila) and Purushpura (Puruṣapura i.e. Peshawar), on either side of the Sindhu River, were connected with the Indian trade route on Indian side and Central Asian trade route on the other. Takshashila, strategically located capital city of Çandhar, was the terminus of several major inland routes and the starting point of the great trade routes connecting India and Central Asia. The Western route from Takshashila passed through Pushkalavati, Purushapura (Peshavar), and Kapisha (Kapiśa, modern Begram) to Bactria (Balkh; Bahlika, Sanskrita). The route from Kapisha to Bactria ran through Bamiyan and a number of passes — Robat, Dandan, Shikan and Karakotal; followed Dana Yousouf river route to reach Majar-i-Sarif and then Bactria. This was the oldest and the most frequented route. Hiuen Tsang, after reaching Bactria from Samarkand, followed this route to reach Bamiyan, Kapisha and Purushapura through Khaibar pass. The importance of Takshashila-Kapisha-Bactria route increased during Achaemenian period when Panjab was its satrapy and during Seleucid period when it became royal highway to the west.

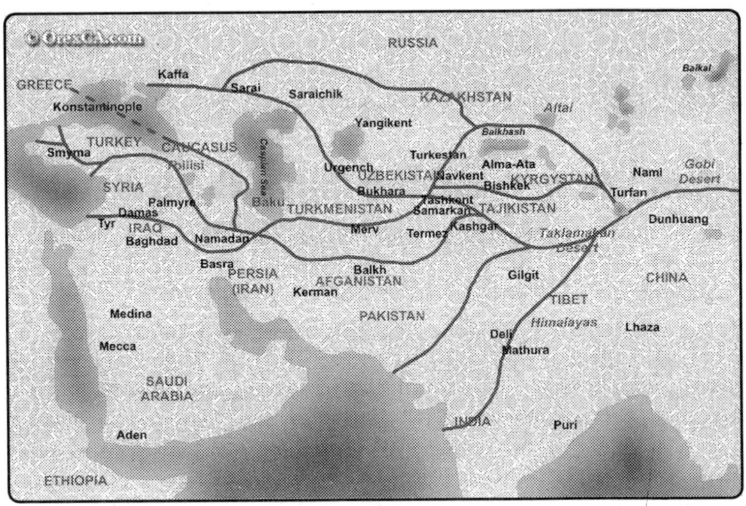

Two routes connected Bactria to the Oxus valley. Strabo, Pliny and other geographers have mentioned about Caspian Highway going towards the Caspian Sea. Indians favoured this route for trade to the Black Sea ports taking advantage of the navigability of Oxus river. The route from Bactria to Samarkand and Tashkent went further to the north-east to Turfan. Tashkent-Turfan route, passing through the northern parts of Tien Shan mountain range, went *via* Kulja and Urumchi cities. Khojend is located about 150 miles south-east of Tashkent.[2] Alexander suffered a military disaster while passing through Samarkand or Marchanda. He went up to Khojend, known as Alexandria Eschate (farthest) at that time.[3]

A northern route, linking India and Central Asia, passed through Kashmir valley to Gilgit, and then to Yarkand and Kashgarh in Eastern Turkistan. Kashgarh also known as *Kashi,* being a centre of Sanskrit learning, was also linked to India *via* Bactria through a route passing south of Pamir. Hiuen Tsang in 644 A.D. for his return journey from India to China and Marco Polo for his journey to Cathay in 1273 A.D. used the same. Passing from Bactria to Badakshan up to the open valley of Wakkan, the road used to go to Sariqol south of the peak Muz Tagh Ata, and then to Tashkurgan and finally, descending the hills to the Kashgarh and Yarkand. A route from Kashmir valley through Gilgit, Darkot and Baroghil passes met Badakhshan-Wakkan-Sariqol route at Sarhad.[4]

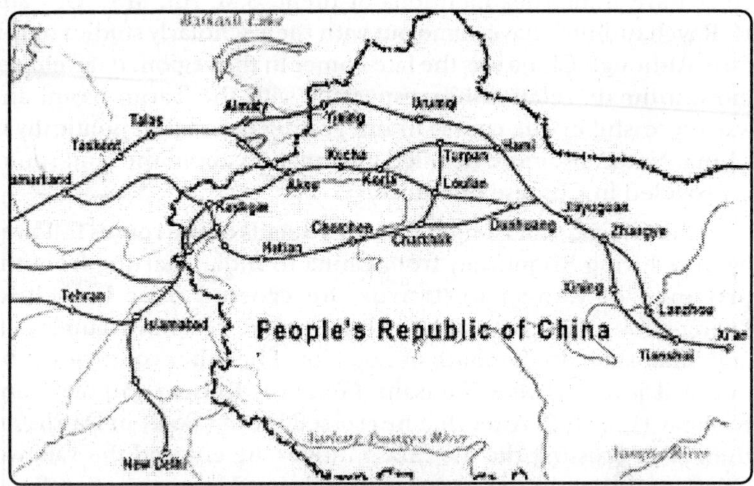

Kashgarh on the western fringe of the Taklamakan desert in Tarim basin of Xinjiang (Chinese Turkistan or Eastern Turkistan), located in between the Tien Shan mountain range in the north and Kun-lun mountain range in the south, was an important trade centre. Two routes, northern and southern emerging from Kashgarh, passed through the important locations in the series of oases on the outer periphery of the oval shaped trough-like Tarim basin desert. Important places on the southern route, passing through the southern periphery of the desert on the northern foot-hills of Kun-lun, were Yarkand, Khotan, Karghalik, Keriya, Niya, Endere, Charchan, Charkhlik and Miran, and after skirting the salty Lop-nor marsh, Tun-huang and An-hsi. The northern route, on the northern periphery south of Tien Shan, passed through Uch Turfan, Aksu, Kucha and Korla. The route bifurcated at Korla towards south-east and north-east. The former route passed through Kuruk Darya, Lou-lan, etc., and terminated at Tun-huang. Karashahr and Turfan were located on north-eastern route. The route made a great arch through Hami, and then ended at An-hsi.[5]

Tashkent-Kurla-Urumchi route met Akshu-Kucha-Karashahr route at Turfan. Huen Tsang followed Hami-Turfan-Tashkent-Samarkand road, and then descended from Oxus valley to Bactria in his onward journey to India.[6]

As discussed elsewhere, the Indians had intimate knowledge about the Central Asian region and its people. The *Purāṇas* and epics have numerous mentions of them. S.M. Ali, M.L. Dev and H. Raychaudhuri[7] have come out with their scholarly studies in this case. Although China was the late-comer in the region, it developed more intimate relationship, especially with the Tarim basin, and was successful in due course in integrating the region politically in China. Naturally, more detailed information about the land routes is provided in Chinese literature.

Chinese pilgrim Fa-hien provides details of the routes followed by him during his journey from China to India. Starting from the province of Kan-su westwards, he crossed over Lan-chou, Leang-chou, Kan-chou and Su-chou, before reaching Tun-huang and Shan-shan, to the south of Lop-Nor. The other countries in his outward journey were Karasahr (Yen-ki,), Khotan (Yu-tien) and Kashgar (Kie-cha). After that he crossed Darel (To-li) in Dardistan; then after crossing the mountain ranges, he entered the valley of Gilgit, and then in the region of the Indus. His co-traveller, Song-yun, however, followed the southern route up to Pamir region — Tash-kurghan (Tsiu-mo) to Wakkan (Pa-ho), then the mountainous region to the north of Chitral (Po-che) to She-ni, and then moving southwards to Udyana in Swat valley, and finally to Gandhar (Peshawar).[8]

Hiuen-Tsang, in his journey up to Bactria, followed northern route. Starting from Kan-su, he went to Yarkhoto (near Turfan; Kao-chang), and then the countries of Karasahr (A-ki-ni), Kucha (Kiu-che) and Yaka-aryk (Po-lo-kia) on the south of Tien-shan mountain range. After that he crossed that mountain range by Bedal pass.[9] The route from Bedal pass to the southern shores of Issyk kul lake in the northern Kyrghyz Republic, passes through the Seok-pass, Arabel valley, Sari Moinok, Barskoon pass, through Barskoon river valley. From south-western shores of the lake, it crosses Boom Gorge; reaches Chu valley and the Suyab region. Here, it needs mention that the road passing through the southern shores of Issyk Kul Lake used to be called 'Hiuen Tsiang Road.'[10] Hiuen Tsang, then passed by Sogdiana (Samarkand), crossed 'Iron Gate' to the south of Kesh (Sahar-i-sabz) and then reached Tokharestan with its capital Kunduz (Huo) to the south of the Oxus before his onwards journey towards Bamiyan.[11] The pilgrim, in his return journey, as mentioned earlier, followed southern route from Kapisha, crossed Hindu Kush by the valley of Panjshir; passed through Kunduz, Badakshan (Pa-to-chuang-na), Yamgan (Yung-po-kien) and Kundut (Hun-to-lo). After that, he crossed Pamir, visited the countries of Tash-Kurgan (Kie-pan-to), Kasghar (Ki-she), Karghalik (Che-Kiu-kia), Khotan (Kiu-sa-tan-na) and followed the usual route through south of Lop-nor to reach Chang-an.[12]

India was also linked up with Tarim basin (Xinjiang) through Ladakh. Ellsworth Huntington followed the route during his journey to that region. In spite of the extreme climate of Karakorum plateau — its higher altitude, extremely windy uncertain climate and the landscape covered with snow, he found traders and Muslim pilgrims going to Makka through India following this route.[13] Huntington, during his journey through Karakorum, found skeletons of dead travellers and animals and bundles of goods scattered throughout the route, which none picked up.[14] He writes about the same:

"On the first day after joining the main caravan road in this region, I counted the remains of thirty-two horses, half eaten by wolves and ravens. The following day in eighteen miles I counted two hundred and twenty skeletons and carcasses of animals that must have died within the last two or three years. We also passed, that day, thirty-six bales of tea, spices, cloth, and Korans, abandoned the previous fall by a caravan which started too late from Leh.... one horse gave out here, two there, and three in another place; then a snow-storm came on, and the men fled for their lives, leaving the remaining loads, ropes and all, in the mid of the flood-plain of a stream. The owner expected to send a new caravan in a month or two to get the goods and carry them to Yarkand. He knew that they would be safe, for such incidents are common. Customs, stronger than law, binds all travellers to respect the property thus temporarily left in the road. We camped at an elevation of 17400 feet, near twelve of the bales, which our men used as wind-break, unmindful of the carcasses of four or five horses lying close at hand."[15]

He further writes:

"We had now reached the centre of the plateau. The next day, June 2, we crossed the Karakorum pass 18300 feet above the sea, the culminating point of the highest trade route in the world. In twenty-one miles, I counted four hundred and seventy-four dead horses, not to mention numerous dismembered skeletons, thirty-two bales of merchandise, and one human corpse."[16]

In spite of enormous difficulty, the route was preferred by many people of Tarim Basin region. He writes about the route:

"Chinese Turkistan is connected with the outside world, other than China, by two routes, those of Karakorum and Terek Davan. The latter runs westward from Kashgar, at the western extremity of the country, to Osh and Andizhan, the terminus of the Central Asian railroad to Russian Turkistan. Since the completion of the railroad, it has largely supplanted the Karakorum route as an avenue for the importation of the manufactured products of Europe. In every way it is an easier route than the other, for it rises to an elevation of only about 12,000 feet, and the part at a high altitude can be crossed in a day or two. In the past, however, as now, communication with the West by this route, more frequently than by the other, must have been interrupted by wars, during which travellers and merchants were forced to use the harder, but cheaper and more peaceful Karakorum route.[17]

He further writes: "Even lately, so remote a geographic impulse as the disorder created by the struggle of the competing nations of Russia and Japan for the coast of the Pacific has outbalanced the influence of the Central Asian railroad, and has turned considerable traffic to Karakorum. When we were at Ladakh, the price of horses and grain showed symptoms of rising, because it became known that about fifteen hundred Muhammedan pilgrims returning from Mecca to their homes in Chinese Turkistan were coming up through India to Leh."[18] Of course, many preferred this route to avoid official harassment during the journey by Russian officials.[19]

As discussed above, India was linked up to the West and to China through Central Asian land route. But, it has direct links with the West through neighbouring Middle-East, Iran and Mesopotamia, as well as with China through land route *via* North-East India, apart from the sea-route linkages. There was an ancient land route from Peshawar to Parvatipur (now in Bangladesh) passing through Vazirabad, Lahour, Jalandhar, Saharanpur, Lucknow, Tirhut and Katihar,[20] which extended further to Assam from Parvatipur.[21] The route mostly passed keeping Ganges to the south. A southern route from Lahour to Bhagalpur through Raivind, Firozpur, Bhatinda, Delhi, Allahabad, Varanasi and Patna, branched off to Ganga Sagar (Calcutta) from Patna. It further extended from Bhagalpur to Kajangal and Rajmahal and then to Calcutta.[22]

Another route branched off from the same to Kamarupa after crossing Ganges at Rajmahal. Bhashkar Burman, the king of Kamarupa and Chinese pilgrim Hiuen Tsang used the same route to come to Kajangal to meet Emperor Harsha there.[23] While coming back to Kanauj from Kajangal, Harsha, with his army, followed the southern and Bhashkar Burman, along with his army and Hiuen Tsang, followed the northern route.[24] The route to Kamarupa further extended to Yunnan province of China *via* north Myanmar.[25] An alternative land route, it needs mention, also existed *via* Chumbi valley of Sikkim and Lhasa (Tibet) to China.[26]

The network of continental land routes, discussed above, linking east to west and north to south, is termed 'Silk Road'. An international seminar held in Japan in 1988 used the term 'Silk Roads', which included both the continental and the maritime routes linking east and the west.[27] The nomenclature, Silk Road, however, ignores the fact that silk was an item of diplomacy for the Chinese, rather than of the trade, and very less silk was left in China after domestic consumption for export. Moreover, India was an equally important partner in the production and trade of Silk. The importance of continental route, however, declined after the discovery of the maritime route linking Europe to India encircling South Africa.

Indian linkages to Central India, especially to the regions of Merv and areas near Çaspian Sea were also through Baluchistan and Iran.[28] The combined sea and land route through Persian Gulf was also in operation.[29] Pilgrims of Ferghana to Mecca travelled through Hindustan as mentioned by Babur.[30]

Two points, which will be discussed elsewhere in the book, need mention before closing the chapter that Buddhism flourished in most of the places/countries visited by traders and the pilgrims. The route, labelled as the Silk Route, was in reality the 'Sutra Route'[31] or the "Jade Route'. After all Buddhism and the Sutras were enthusiastically patronized by the Turk chieftains also.

References

1. Banerjee, P.; Hindu Deities in Central Asia, in *India's Contribution to World Thought and Culture*, pp. 281-87.
2. *Ibid.*, p. 110.
3. *The Cultural Heritage of India*, Vol. VI, pp.221-223. Calcutta, (1991).

4. *Ibid.*, p. 223.
5. *Ibid.*, pp. 223-24.
6. *Ibid.*
7. S.M. Ali's *The Geography of the Purāṇas*, New Delhi (1996), N.L. Dev's *The Geography Dictionary : Ancient and Medieval India*, London (1927) and H. Raychaudhuri's *Studies in Indian Antiquities*, Calcutta (1932) used to be path-breaking studies in this direction.
8. Puri, B.N., *Buddhism in Central Asia*, Delhi (2000); p. 17, n. 20.
9. *Ibid.*
10. World Heritage Convention, *Silk Road Sites in Kyrghyzstan*; Report submitted by the National Commission of the Kyrghyz Republic for the UNESCO; 19.2.2010.
11. Puri, *op. cit.*, pp. 17-18.
12. *Ibid.*, p. 18; Prabodh Chandra Bagchi, *India and Central Asia*, p. 17.
13. Huntington, Ellsworth, *The Pulse of Asia*, Boston and New York; pp. 47-90.
14. *Ibid.*, p. 83.
15. *Ibid.*
16. *Ibid.*
17. *Ibid.*, p. 87.
18. *Ibid.*, pp. 87-88.
19. *Ibid.*, p. 88.
20. Dr. Motichandra, *Sarthavaha*, Patna (1953); p. 12.
21. *Ibid.*
22. *Ibid.*
23. Vasu, N.N.; *Social History of Kamarupa*, Vol. 1; p. 151.
24. *Ibid.*
25. Motichandra, op. cit., p. 127.
26. Kumar, B.B.; *The Border Trade in North-East India: The Historical Perspective*, in 'Border Trade: North-East India and Neighbouring Countries'; Gurudas Das and R.K. Purkayastha (Ed.), New Delhi (2000); pp. 1-2.
27. Tadao Umesao and Toh Sugimara (Ed.); *Significance of Silk Roads in Human Civilization*, Osaka (1992).
28. Mason, V.M.; Paper presented in the Seminar on "India and Central Asia".
29. *The Cultural Heritage of India*, Vol. VI, pp. 224-25.
30. *Baburnama*, Hindi tr. By Yugjit Navapuri; Sahitya Akademy, New Delhi, 2002; p. 11.
31. Bagchi, P.C.; *India and China*; p. 15.

5

Silk, Silk Trade and the Silk Routes

The silk culture originated in China and India in prehistoric time. According to traditional Chinese accounts, the queen of the legendary Chinese emperor Huang-ti, during the third millennium B.C., was credited for the cultivation of silk worm and weaving of silk. It, however, flourished during the period of Shang dynasty (c. 1523-1027 B.C.). But the silk culture remained unknown for the West until 552 A.D., when two Nestorian monks, living in China, brought small quantity of silkworm eggs, concealed in their palmer staves, to Constantinople. The sericulture spread in the West Asia and Europe only after that.[1] There is also a similar legend of smuggling of silkworm eggs by a Chinese princess married to the king of Khotan. The legend of famous silk princess, who secretly introduced the silk worm culture in Khotan, is depicted in a wooden tablet of Khotan.... The four-armed figure has two of the attributes of the Iranian Bodhisattva, the cup and the knife with a short triangular blade, and both are wearing a crown.[2] The silk princess votive Tablet from Dandan Uiliq (Khotan, is now in the British Museum, London[3]). With minor variation, similar images to earlier one, are found on number of Panels in Dandam Uiliq.[4]

In India, a particular category of silk was known as *cinamshuka* or *cinapatta,* which clearly indicated its Chinese origin. However, there were other silk varieties with Indian linkages, *Tasar,* for example, originated in North-East India, and dispersed from the same to South-East Asia, China and Japan. In this connection, it is relevant to bring to notice the Japanese legend of the "Princess with Golden Hair". It is the legend of a princess of *Madhyadeśa,* India, *"l'empire du milieu de l'Inde".* After her survived from "a series of harrowing incidents engineered by her wicked step-mother, the princess finally emerged in Japan, where she died, transforming herself in the process, into a silkworm which spun yellow silk. Pariset reads the legend at several levels as reflecting the life history in allegorical terms of the silkworm spinning yellow silk and the geographical dispersion of this worm through China to Japan." He, however, identifies the filament as *Bombyx Mori,* the Chinese term for which is *Kin-cul-tsan,* meaning 'the child with the cover of gold. The dating suggested, based on the sign for kin, meaning golden, is dated to *circa* eighth century B.C.[5]

The history of production and use of silk in China and India goes back to the remote past. The earliest evidence of the silk and silk fabrics was found in the archaeological discovery of the Liangzhu civilization of China existing in *circa* 3000 B.C.[6] In India, the twine of white silk fibre, spun from cut cocoons, used for stringing beads dated *circa* 1500-1000 B.C. was found at the excavations of Nevasa in Ahmednagar district.[7] The sample of the woven silk was found in the excavation in a relic casket at Devni Mori, Sabarkantha district, Gujarat dated *circa* 375 A.D. to the reign of the Kshatrapa king Rudrasen.[8] Here it needs to be pointed out that silk finds numerous mentions in Indian literature.

As we know, silk is produced from the cocoons produced by the silky secretion of the silkworm caterpillar; the colour and texture of the silk produced by different kinds of moths and their feed, i.e. host-plants, differs. Here, it needs mention that there are two varieties of silk producing lepidopterist insects, namely Bombycidae and Saturnidae, out of which only one variety of the former category, *Bombyx mori* produce silk, whereas insects of the latter category, namely *Antheraea assamensis, philosamia ricini* and *A. mylitta* produce *muga, eri* and *tasar* respectively. Now the silkworm moth may be fully domesticated, such as *B. Mori* in China. But there are in India different kinds of silk with different names, and differing in texture and colours—*tasara, muga, eri, pat*—produced in different parts of the country.[9] The silkworm in China feeds on mulberry, which is also an important host plant in India. It is a sub-Himalayan Indian tree, which has also been grown traditionally in China and Japan.[10] *Naga* tree (*Keseru; Heteropanax fragrans)* hosts *eri* worm; *Champaka (Michelia champaka)* hosts *muga* worm, *A. assamensis.* Another wild silkworm, *A. mezankooria,* Moore, also yields white silk muga, when fed on *Mejankeri, Litsaea cirtrata, L. cubeba,* Perb. Likuca tree (*A. Lakoocha)* host to the wild silkworm moths, *B. (T.) bengalensis,* Hutton and *T. affins,* Hutton of Bengal and Chota Nagpur (Now Jharkhand) respectively. Bakula tree *Mimuseps elengi)* is host to the wild moth

Trilocha varians, Walker or *Ocinaravarians,* Hamps. Again, *T. religiosae,* Helfer feeds on the banyan tree (*Ficus Indica*).[11] Here, it needs mention that the term *eri,* for a kind of silk produced in India, is derived from Sanskrit term *errand* (Hindi, *rendi*), a particular silkworm feeder plant. *Champak, Lakuch* and *Bakula,* the names of feeder plants, are also the Sanskrit terms. Banyan, as the name *Ficus Indica* indicates, is an Indian tree.

Tasar is Magadhi/Ardhamagadhi term, meaning thread; Sanskrit and Pali word *tasar,* it needs mention, means 'a shuttle of a loom'. In Rajashekhara's *Karpuramanjari,* the term is used in the sense of 'coarse silk'. Turner gives the meaning of Prakrit work *tasar,* "a kind of thread".[12] For silk, the term used in Sanskrit is *kausheya,* derived from *kosha* meaning cocoon. Panini, of fifth century B.C., uses the term *koshad*[13] and Patanjali, of second century B.C., *krimau* (Sanskrit *krimi* means worm) for silkworm.[14] Here, it needs mention that mulberry. *Morus indica,* uses to be the most important feeder tree for the silkworm, for which we have term in different languages :Hindi—*tut, sahatut;* Bengali—*tunt;* Marathi—*tutai;* Gujarati—*shetur.* The Sanskrit terms for mulberry are *tula*[15] *tuta, tuda, brahmakashta, kramuka* and *kramukh* (Monier Williams identifies the term with mulberry). *Kṛmijatanam* is silk cloth in *Arthasāshtra.*[16] *Yuktikalpataru* discusses various categories of silk and silkworm; it classified silkworm into four, namely Brāhmana, Kshatriya, Vaishya and Shudra categories.

In India, the silk and sericulture has linkages with numerous regions and communities. The most important regions of silk production, however, are the North-East and eastern regions, especially Assam and Bengal. However, it has been produced since ancient days in Bihar, Jharkhand, Orissa and Karnataka also. The most important community producing silk are the Bodos of Assam. Suniti Kumar Chatterji, wrongly, attributes their origin to Central Asia, which for years continued to be Sanskritist region, according to Toyanbee and not the Tibeto-Burman one. The rearing and weaving of Assam *pat,* a fine white silk of Bombyx variety, was confined to Katani Jugis, a weaving community driven out of Bengal by Ballal Sen (1159-1179 A.D.). This silk was used by Assam royalty. Pundas were yet the other hereditary silkworm rearing caste of Bengal.

Though production of silk started in China and India, there

was diffusion of the knowledge, gradually, to different parts of the world. The silk industry was set up in a large number of countries. But there was decline of silk industry in many countries due to discovery and use of rayon.

The silk has given name to the land routes linking China, India and Europe through Central Asia. The entire focus on such nomenclature is based on the assumption that silk was the most important item of trade through Central Asia, and China was the most important player in the same. The reality is that (i) silk was an item of diplomacy, rather than the trade for the China; and (ii) China was a late comer, as well as a minor player, on Central Asian stage through which the so called Silk Route passes. The Chinese emperor, Wu-ti (140—87 B.C.) sent his envoy Chang-kyan for the first time to Central Asia to collect first hand information about the region only during 128 B.C., whereas Professor Arnold Toynbee asserted, the Sanskrit speaking people dominated the scene since eighteenth century B.C. to fourth century A.D.[17] Another factor which needs to be kept in mind in this case is that China hardly produced enough silk for trade after meeting its domestic needs; its production also used to be comparatively small.

The silk production was small in China up to 1125 B.C. The usage was mainly restricted then for standards and parasols.[18] The rise of steppe nomadism and conflict with the Hunas further restricted the westward contact ; nd China's trade prospect up to initial centuries of Christian era. But Chinese objects like silk, mirrors and lacquer were found in the graves of the nomad warrior aristocracy. This, of course, might have been obtained in small quantities through raids, warfare, tributes, gift exchange, and, of course, limited trade. It is an accepted fact that silk might have acquired some symbolic value, necessitating its use in the grave.[19]

In China, silk has a linkage with royalty and courtly privilege since antiquity. It was used in gift exchange and in payment for royal services rendered. Silken robes were used only by the high ups. Silk fabric was an essential item to be given by the Chinese state to the Huns and other nomads as per the treaty conditions between them. At times, China used to send silk to the Hun, Turk and Uigur chieftains as either annual tribute or to meet their unjust demands.[20] China, even as late as early decades of eleventh century A.D., paid three lakh bales of silk and two lakh ounce (156 mounds) of silver as annual tribute to the Khittan chief[21] apart from other humiliating terms and conditions imposed on Chinese emperor.

In China the commoners were termed *pu-i,* as they were prevented from wearing silken cloth and used to wear only *pu* (a generic term for non silken fabric). Thus, higher internal use and limited production, as mentioned above, restricted the availability of silk for trade. Moreover, the silk production was a state monopoly during Han period. But, silk was certainly an item limited of export for the Chinese, which is evident from the Greek and Roman appellation of *Seres* for China derived from the kingdom of Shu, in present day Sichuan. Here it needs mention that the Chinese ideograph for Shu is a silkworm. In this case, China for its neighbours was either "Middle Kingdom; *Chung kuo"* (Japanese, *Tsiou kokue;* Burmese, *Alai prai dai;* Mongol, *Doumda-iin oulous*; Manchu, *Doulimba-I Gouroun;* Tongkingese, *Djoua kwok)* or "Eastern Dawn" *(Chin tan;* Japanese, *Morou Kossi*) or Celestial Empire *(Thian tchhao),* etc. In case *of* India, it is usually presumed that Indian name for China is derived from the name of a particular Chinese dynasty Tsin; which does not seem to be true. Prakrit Persian name for China, having currency in Central Asia also, was Kattaii or Khittai/Khitai, which was derived from Kitan, a dynasty ruling in north China during 1118-1235 A.D. In India, two terms for China—*Cin* in *Arthasashtra; Mahachin* in *Mahabharata*— were in currency. As India had contact with South-west China through Brahmaputra valley and that with North-west China through Central Asia, and at the same time such contacts take us to deeper antiquity, it is probable that the term *Cin* may have linkage either with *Chiang* or *Jiang* (a community of South-west China) or with *Ch'in* or *Ts'in* (a state of ninth century western China).

The silk imported in the Roman West was also known as Assyrian silk; but there was ambiguity in their mind with regard to the identity of Assyria and Syria, and even Syria was itself believed to be close to India. Moreover, silk was also an item originating from India on which taxes were levied by the Romans.[22]

When Chinese envoy Chiang Kyang, sent by Chinese emperor Wu-ti, came to Central Asia to have first hand information about the region and to persuade *Tusharas (Yueh-chis)* to return back to their original homeland, he found Indian and Chinese goods in Bactria brought by Indian traders.[23] The land route system in the region predated its contact with China and the trade of Chinese silk. Moreover, silk, as discussed above was an item of diplomacy for the Chinese, rather than the item of trade. Therefore, the nomenclature "Silk Route" is erroneous. It was, in reality, the *Sutra Route* and *Jade Route.* The opinion of eminent Indian scholar, Professor Lokesh Chandra is relevant; he writes: "The so called Silk Route was really the Path of Sutras over the centuries. This is clear from the decline of this international highway when *sramanas, sutras* and sancta were annihilated by fundamentalist terrorism, the route lost its glorious heritage as well as its flourishing economy."[24] He further writes that "Sanskrit was the very being of the so called 'Silk Route' which should really be called the Sutra Route."[25]

In the context of Central Asia, the fact should always be kept in mind that the region has intimate linkages with India and Iran, being part of the India-Iran-Uttarapath (Central Asia) Cultural-Religious-Trade Continuum zone. Again, Vedic religion/Hinduism preceded Buddhism in the region.

References

1. *Encyclopaedia Americana,* Vol. 25; New York, 1965, edition; p. 1.
2. Stein, *Ancient Khotan,* D, X Pl. LXIII.
3. Puri, B.N., *Buddhism in Central Asia,* p. 273 note.
4. *Ibid.*, p. 273.
5. Varadarajan, Lotika, *Silk — The Extra Silk Route Story,* the paper presented at the International Seminar held at IGNCA, New Delhi on January 17-19, 2003; it refers Pariset, E., *Histoire de Soie,* Lyon (1843), pp.77 79.
6. *Ibid.*
7. Gulati, 1961, pp. 55, 57; quoted by Varadarajan.
8. Mehta, R.N. and S.N. Chaudhury; *Excavation at Devni Mori, A Report of the Excavation Conducted from 1960 to 1963;* Baroda (1966), p.120.
9. Varadarajan, *op. cit.*
10. Sanchez, M.D., *World Distribution and Utilization of Mulberry, Potential for Animal Feeding;* Food and Agriculture Organization Document; Electronic Conference on Mulberry for Animal Production.
11. Varadarajan, *op. cit.*
12. Turner, R.L.; A *Comparative Dictionary of the Indo-Aryan Languages,* OUP, 1966, no. 5744, 27.
13. Panini, *Ashtadhyayi,* 4.3.41.
14. Abhyankar, 1952, 234; quoted by Varadarajan.
15. *Arthashastra,* 14.2.6.8.
16. *Ibid.*, 2.22.6; R.P. Kangle, *The Kautilya Arthasastra, 11,* Bombay (1972), p.145.

17. Toynbee, Professor Arnold J., 'Value of Oriental History for Historians', *The Journal of Siam Society,* Bangkok; October 1957. Quoted by Prof. Raghuvira.
18. Pariset, 1843, pp. 13-15, 21-23; quoted by Varadarajan.
19. Raschke, 1978, pp. 606-611, n. 83; quoted by Varadarajan.
20. Rahul Sankrityayan, *Madhya Asia ka Itihas,* (Hindi), Vol. 1, Patna (1985) pp. 85-86, 244, 246.
21. Rahul Sankrityayan, *op. cit.*, p. 354.
22. Varadarajan, *op. cit.*
23. Rahul Sankrityayan, *op. cit.*, p. 175.
24, Lokesh Chandra, 'Sanskrit on the Silk Route', *Dialogue,* Vol. 15, No. 3.
25. *Ibid.*

6

Nomadism in Central Asia

Central Asia, from the very early days, was inhabited by the nomadic people in the north and sedentary ones in the south. The nomadic zone consists of the northern steppes from South Russia to Manchuria; the region to the south, including oases of the Tarim basin formed sedentary zone. In the nomadic zone the region from South Russia up to the valley of Ienessi was occupied by the Scythians, the nomadic hordes of Aryan stock; on the other hand, Turco-Mongol hordes occupied the region to the east, including 'Outer Mongolia' and 'Inner Mongolia', Manchuria and further east. Again, the region in the south between the Jaxartes (Syr Darya)

Author (1st from left) with Shri K. Santhanam (3rd from l.), Indian Ambassador in Uzbekistan (4th from l.) and members of the India Central Asia Foundation Expedition Team at Shastri Memorial, Tashkent.

and Oxus (Amu Darya) was occupied by the sedentary people of Iranian stock;[1] whereas, the settled inhabitants of the Tarim basin oases were of Indian stock.[2] Toynbee confirms that "from eighteenth century B.C. to fourth century A.D.", the "Sanskrit speaking races, who were "spread from Hungary to North-West fringes of China" dominated Central Asia.[3] In Central Asia, as elsewhere in the world, geography and climate, rather than the race, was the factor responsible for nomadism.

Geography and Climate dictate the Way of Life

In any region of the world, as in Central Asia, the Geography and the climate dictated the way of life. In the North Eurasian region, from South Russia to Manchuria, where summer is short, rain is scanty, the climate is suitable only for the growth of grass; the trees rarely grow there, and that too on river banks. Such grass lands (steppe) are ideal for pastoral nomads. But even the grass at one place is hardly enough for their herds and therefore, the pastoral inhabitants of the steppe region take their herds from place to place for grazing, and thus lead a nomadic life. Under such circumstances, the shepherds have no alternative than to change their residence at least twice in the year and their family members move with them as leaving the women and children far away is not safe. Moreover, it becomes necessary for all members of the family to share the work of looking after the cattle and the sheep and therefore, to move together. Again, as keeping the flocks at only one place makes it dirty and the grass of the nearby area is very soon consumed, the shepherds regularly shift their residences. Thus, the geography and climate are the factors responsible for the nomadic pastoral way of living in the northern steppe region of Central Asia, as the aridity makes agriculture difficult. At the same time, scanty shifting population and distance from the sea does not allow the growth of trade centres.

Like the nomadism in northern Eurasia, the Kyrghyz of the Tian Shan plateau and the tribes of Pamir also lead nomadic life due to the same factors. In eastern Central Asia, the most important geographical feature of the Tian Shan plateau are the plains of rich grass, or the 'pamirs', as they are generally called. The climate of the region is too cold; the snow lasts too long, making it impossible for the men and animals to reside there permanently. Under such extreme conditions, innumerable marmots hibernate; the birds

A Hill Side in Central Asia

Yurt in a Valley

migrate, as it is difficult for them to find food there due to scarcity of insects and as the weeds have large seeds. However, the conditions become ideal for the pastoral nomads after the melting of snow, due to the availability of abundant grass for millions of herbivorous sheep and cattle. Then, during summer months, there is abundant growth of thick, turfy grass full of flowers in the rich grassy upland; millions of sheep and cattle graze there and get fattened. But the nomads have to conduct several days journey to drive down their flocks back to the dry plains or to the protected valleys before the winter sets in. The family members work together to dismantle and shift their movable residences, *Yurts* or *Kibitkas.*[4]

Climate Change and the Forced Migration

The climate change is a known and accepted fact today. The periodic variation in climate takes place usually after about 36 years, as Bruckner has shown; severer climate changes are reported after the long gap. As such, there was world-wide dry period during 1830-40, 1865-1875 and 1887-99; which was not without adverse effect on the population worldwide. During the first epoch of dry spell in the Lop basin of Chinese Turkistan, the villages of Dumuka, Ponak and others were abandoned for lack of water; and new villages were founded at higher upstreams. At other places such movements led to the founding of the villages of Niya, Cherchen and Charclick.

Mountain and the Valley

During the next two periods of dry spell of climate, there was rebellion among Dungans and others.[5] Here, it needs mention that even the climate change at one place adversely effected the population elsewhere, as it happened in Turfan. The direct cause of the depopulation of the densely populated prosperous villages of Turfan, two hundred years earlier, was not the scarcity of water, but the raids of plundering Mongol nomads from the surrounding mountains. The Mongols felt the pinch after the mountains, with more moisture and vegetation, became too dry for habitation; their cattle and flocks started dwindling. The phase of comparative peace with their neighbours ended. Despising agriculture, they did not change to sedentary habits; moved further displacing others and depopulating other areas.[6] Thus, the climate change at one place adversely affected the people living elsewhere. In this connection, it needs mention that the changes mentioned above are not restricted to Lop basin and Turfan only. Different regions of the world undergo climate change either at regular intervals or after a long period. Various regions of the world have the records of desiccation and cooling, as well as that of more rain and warming. Whereas desiccation brings abandonment of settled areas and forced migration, the changes, such as, increase in rain, catalyze population growth. The vast plains of Central Asia, for example, "appear to have supported untold hordes of nomads. When the plains began to grow, rapidly drier, the inhabitants must have suffered sorely."[7] Huntington quotes Hahn, providing relevant information about the decreasing capacity of the land to support the herds under drier conditions:

"According to Hahn, a rainfall of twenty inches a year in New South Wales makes it possible to keep over six hundred sheep on a square mile of land; with a rainfall of thirteen inches only a hundred can be kept; and with ten inches only ten sheep. During the short space of thirty-six years cycle, meteorological records show that the rainfall at certain Siberian stations near the centre of Asia may vary in the ratio of two and three tenths in the good years to one in the bad years. Therefore, we can scarcely be exaggerating if we assume that during the great and relatively sudden desiccation in the early part of our era, the average rainfall decreased in the ratio of two to one."[8]

The result of such climate change, as he further writes, was bound to be disastrous leading to unprecedented migration of the nomads:

"If it fell from thirteen inches to six or seven inches, the nomads would have been able to find pasture for only one sheep where formerly they found it for fifteen. If the rainfall fell from twenty inches to ten, the number of sheep would decrease from sixty to one. Manifestly, if such a change took place in the course of few hundred years, most of the inhabitants would be obliged to migrate."[9]

Here, it needs mention that the disastrous impact of desiccation is equally felt by the agricultural communities globally everywhere. But it is felt more severely in Central Asia due to geographical and climatic factors. In Chinese Turkistan, increasing aridity not only resulted in driving away the nomads; the number of persons depending on agriculture too highly decreased and people were reduced to lower stage of civilization. At places like Endereh, Yartungaz, Lulan and elsewhere, the population disastrously decreased and the remaining few people were compelled to abandon agriculture and to adopt the life of semi-nomadic shepherds or fishermen. Thus, higher aridity resulted into high reduction in population. In the north too, it was the rapid increase in aridity which forced the Mongols out of the mountains; 'the wandering nomads raided their neighbours in the villages of the plains so mercilessly as to drive away practically the whole population.' In the arid region everywhere, one finds 'evidence that desiccation has caused famines, depopulation, raids, wars, migrations, and decay of civilization.'[10] In this case, it needs mention that enormous proof of frequent climate changes have been found in Central Asia.[11]

Thus, the climate and geography determined the history of Central Asia leading to nomadic way of life. But even in the southern sedentary zone, the comparative aridity made the agriculture and sedentary way of life difficult. The nomadic horse riders dominated the region for millennia and only few major cities developed in the region.

Conflict between Nomads and the Sedentary People

The conflict between the steppe nomads and sedentary dwellers was a regular affair in Central Asia and its neighbouring countries. Apart from intra-regional and intra-community conflicts and ethnic changes within Central Asia, the conflicts with the Central Asian nomads changed the course of history of not only China, India and Iran, but that of Europe also. Nomads gave China two dynasties; forced that country to build China Wall. Huns, Turks, and lastly Khittans, used to impose humiliating terms on Chinese emperors and exact tributes in spite of regular depredations in Chinese territories. Even as late as in the initial decades of eleventh century China had to pay two lakh ounces of silver and three lakh bales of silk to the Khittans; and even then the most barbaric depredations by the Khittans continued on the Chinese territory.[12]

War Technique and Strength of the Nomads

It needs mention here that the nomadic lifestyle was comparatively well-suited to warfare due to the devastating techniques, and ability and skill of warfare developed by them.[13] The nomadic Scythian horsemen developed the saddle; with the Alans, the use of stirrup became common. As the horses grew larger and sturdier to carry the warriors with ease, the mobility of the nomads highly increased and the use of chariot became unnecessary. The nomads developed the skill of using the bow from the horse-back. Almost the entire men population, from a young age, was trained in riding and archery, the skills necessary for survival in the steppe. By the time a nomad achieved adulthood, such activities became his second nature, making an archer capable of easily travelling forty miles per day. Thus the nomads were quick to dominate Central Asia and to exact tribute from the scattered city states under the threat of their annihilation.

The Huns developed a war technique of posing before their enemies of being defeated, running away from the war field, and thus tempting their enemies to pursue them, take them deep in their area; and then encircle, fight and defeat them. Using this technique, Maudun, the Hun king, defeated a Chinese army of three lakh army men. The Chinese monarch, somehow, escaped. China was forced to give a Chinese princess, silk, precious stones, jewels, rice, wine and different kinds of food items as tribute to the Huns.[14]

The different nomadic groups, at times, formed confederations under a single ruler (khan) and acted in unison, making them most powerful. In such a case, their actions became most devastating as it happened when the Huns arrived in Western Europe. Turk Khan, Mo-cho (693-716 A.D.) could build 3,000 miles long empire, stretching from Central Asia to Korea.[15] When Genghis Khan united different tribes of Mongolia and used superior military techniques, the most spectacular power could emerge in the Central Asia comprising the entire China, Central Asia, parts of Russia and the Middle East. Successor Chagatai Khanate continued to control the region after the death of Genghis Khan in 1227, and then disintegrated. In 1369, Timurlane, a Turkic leader of the Mongol military tradition, conquered most of the region. Timur's large empire, however, collapsed just after his death leading to the division of the same into Khanates of Khiva, Bukhara, Kokand and Kashgar. Earlier, during sixth and seventh centuries, the Hephthalites, the most powerful among the nomad groups of the region, controlled much of the Central Asia. The region was divided between powerful states of the Seljuk Turks, Samanid dynasty, Khwarizmi Empire and others during tenth and eleventh centuries.

The nomadic states, however, proved to be short-lived due to certain internal weaknesses. As per the tradition, the conquered dominion used to be divided among the Khan's sons; this resulted into lack of centralized power of control. Moreover, it was easier to conquer the non-nomadic people than to govern them, as for governing the sedentary people, the nomads had to rely on the local bureaucracy. This was essential as the diffused political structure of the nomadic steppe confederacies was inadequate and mal-adjusted to the complex states of the settled people. Moreover, reliance on the alien bureaucracy led to the rapid assimilation of the nomads into the culture of the former. Here, it needs mention that during Timur's reign, due to the same reason, the nomadic steppe culture of the Central Asia fused with the sedentary culture of Iran.

Again, there was another difficulty for them. As the steppe army depended solely on the horses — each warrior needing three to four horses — their maintenance for longer period was only possible in the steppes, where the large stretches of grazing land were available. Apart from this limiting factor, yet another limiting factor for the army of the nomads was their inability to penetrate the dense forested regions to the north, due to which states like Novgorod and Muscovy could grow and become very powerful in due course. Thus becoming powerful, Russian state gradually controlled Western Central Asia; incorporated it into Russian Empire, and subsequently into USSR. Thus geography and climate change were also responsible for moulding the history of the region, as well for the pastoral nomadism and migrations leading to ethnic change in Central Asia.

Strength of the Nomads

The strength of the nomads of Central Asia lied in nomadism itself is evident from the advice of Ton-Yu-Kuk, one of the advisers of Mo-gi-lyan, the Turk kagan (khan/king; 716-735 A.D.) against kagan's wish to construct protected townships and Buddhist *viharas.* He said:

"No, the population of Turks is insignificant; that is not even one per cent of the Chinese population. The only reason of proving our strength before China lies in our being nomadic; we can carry our rations on our Sholdiers and each of us is expert in the art of warfare. We go on plundering expeditions after gaining strength and hide somewhere when we become weak, where it is not possible for China to catch us. If we start settling in towns and changing our way of living, then very soon, we may lose our freedom. These Buddhist *viharas* and temples make people soft. But, only those may keep human-race under control, who are terrible and warriors."[16]

Nomadism with a Difference

Alexander, when he came to the Central Asia, found that neither the cities nor the villages were having the protective walls, although their neighbours, Shakas were also nomads.[17] On the other hand, Chang Kyang, the Chinese envoy, coming to the region two hundred years after him in 128 B.C., found even the villages well-protected. Bagchi notes the same and writes:

"Although there had been earlier movements of the Scythian hordes from the Central Asian steppes to the West. The sedentary civilization of China, Central Asia, Persia and India do not seem to have been affected much by such movements before the third century B.C."[18]

Situational Change and Race Migration

As noted above, the situation changed after third century B.C. The race migration from Mongolian deserts forced race migration elsewhere also. Bagchi further writes:

"Since then the movements became continuous till the times of great Mongol invasions, and affected the civilization of almost the whole of sedentary Asia. Most of these race movements started from the Mongolian deserts, and set in motion all the nomadic tribes in the West."[19]

The Factors Responsible

This must have been due to difference in the behavioural pattern of the nomadic Shakas and the Huns. The Shaka nomads, having more intimate time-depth cultural, linguistic, economic and religious links with their sedentary neighbours in the southern Central Asia, Indians and Iranians, than the Huns, developed different behavioural pattern than that of the latter. The behavioural pattern of the Huns, on the other hand, was moulded during centuries of their conflict with China; their raids and depredations in Chinese territory; exacting heavy tributes from the latter, became second nature for them. The change came only due to construction of China Wall, and gradual weakening of the Hun power due to Chinese policy of dividing, weakening and militarily defeating the Huns. The direction of Hun movement towards south was turned to the west and south-west.

Nomadism in the Civilizational Framework

There are many myths and lies, persisting among our scholars due to colonial hang-over, which create perceptional haziness among them. The Central Asian study is not free from the same. One such myth, persisting among the scholars, is that nomads are barbaric and down in the civilizational scale. The reality is that nomads were as civilized or barbaric as others. Nomad's dependence, especially in Central Asia, on a profession requiring movement from one place to another, was only due to restrictions imposed by geography and climate, but it did not limit their capacity to develop metallurgy. The finds in the graves of the nomads of Altai and Tian Shan attest to the higher civilization of the nomads.

End of Nomad Dominance

The discovery of firearms in the sixteenth century allowed settled people to gain control of the region. Russia and China expanded and could control most of the Central Asia. The nomad dominance ended as a result of the new discoveries, such as, of gun-powder. At the same time, the area with settled population gradually increased. The last decade of the twentieth century witnessed the birth of five independent states in Central Asia.

References

1. Bagchi, Prabodh Chandra; *India and Central Asia,* Calcutta (1955), p. 1.
2. *Ibid.*, Huntington, Ellsworth, *The Pulse of Asia, A Journey in Central Asia Illustrating the Geographic Basis of History*; Houghton, Miffin & Company, Boston and New York (1907); p. 139.
3. Toynbee quoted by Prof. Dr. Raghu Vira, 'Our view of the globe', *in India and Asia: A Cultural Symphony*, International Academy of Indian Culture, New Delhi (1978); p. 20.
4. Huntington, *op. cit.*, pp. 108-9.
5. *Ibid.*, pp. 183; 373.
6. *Ibid.*, p. 313
7. *Ibid.*, p. 382.
8. *Ibid.*, pp. 382-83
9. *Ibid.*, p. 383
10. *Ibid.*, p. 378-79.
11. Sankrityayan, Rahul; *Madhya Asia ka Itihas,* (Hindi); Patna (1985); pp. 44-45.
12. *Ibid.*, p. 354.
13. O'Connell, Robert L.; *Soul of the Sword*; The Free Press, New York, 2002; p. 51.
14. Sankrityayan, *op. cit.*, p. 85.
15. Sankrityayan, *op. cit.*, p. 126.
16. *Ibid.*, pp. 128-29.
17. *Ibid.*, pp. 177.
18. Bagchi, Prabhat Kumar, *India and Central Asia*; Calcutta (1955); p. 3.
19. *Ibid.*

7

Religion and Cult Syncretism in Central Asia

The famous Nicolo seal with a four-armed deity, having in his four hands a wheel, a mace, a ring like object and a globular thing, with a devotee standing by his side in respectful pose with folded hands, was described by Cunningham in the *Numismatic Chronicle* as Viṣṇu, the deity and King Huvishka, the attending devotee. The Kushana identity of Huvishka was identified because of the affinities of headdress and garment.[1] Right interpretation of the seal, however, was possible only after correct decipherment of the inscription by R. Ghirsman.[2] The inscription, according to him, was in Tokharian script and in Tokharian language; it contained the names of Mihir (the Sun God), Viṣṇu and Śiva. But the devotee, according to him, was some unknown Hapthalite Chief, rather than the Kushana King Huvishka. Anyway, irrespective of the identity of the devotee, the use of Tokharian script and language made it clear that composite cult of Shiva (*Śiva*), Vishnu (*Viṣṇu*) and Mitra was popular in Central Asia.

The Russian scholar, A.N. Bernshtam, in 1956, discovered in Tajikistan a fragment of Kharosthi inscription. J. Harmatta translated it as *Nārāyaṇa, be victorious*. The inscription, on palaeographic grounds was to be attributed to second-first century B.C. The explanations of the statement, however, differ, as to whether *Nārāyaṇa* is *Viṣṇu,* as in Hindu mythology; or Narayaṇa (*Nārāyaṇa*) the Buddha, as mentioned in the Khotanese-Saka documents; or Narayana, the *deva,* as in Soghdian documents.[3] Before elaborating the matter further it is necessary to mention that Hinduism accepts Buddha as an incarnation, the *avatāra* of Narayana, the Vishnu. Interestingly, we find example of such cult syncretism even in distant Java in Indonesia, a region on other end of the zone of India-centric religious-cultural continuum. In Java, the Sun was identified with Śiva (perhaps also with Viṣṇu) R.C. Majumdar writes:

Dr. Goris has given detailed account of the rites, ceremonies and *mantras* used in connection with *Sūrya-sevana* or the worship of the Sun. It may be noted at the outset that the Sun was identified with Śiva (perhaps also with Viṣṇu) and Sūrya-sevana really means the worship of Śiva in the form of the Sun.[4]

Conceptual Framework : The Roots

For the roots of such cult syncretism, we may go back to *Rig Veda*, which says that 'the truth is one, the learned speak it variously' (*Ekam Sad Viprā Bahudhā Vadanti*).[5] It further says that 'the word is of four kinds; the learned know it; its three parts are unknown; the fourth men speak. That (*Brahma*) is called Indra, Mitra or Varuna; the same is the Sun in the sky, the same is Agni (Fire), Yama and Matarishva (*Mātrisvā*).[6] In Hindu conceptualization, the gods synchronize; One reflects the other; All reflect the Supreme, i.e. Brahma. We find the echo of the same in *Mātri Upanishad.* It says 'He is Brahma, He is Viṣṇu, He is Rudra, Prajapati, Agni, Varuṇa, Vāyu, Indra, Moon, Yama, Earth, He is all.'

The *Rig Veda* re-states the same truth, as given below:

'Kindled in numerous places the fire is one,
Lording over all the sun is one,
The dawn that illuminates this all is one,
And forsooth one is it that variously
Appears as this all.'[7]

It is evident from the above that the concept of the Supreme was the same, at least at the level of the learned society from South-East Asia through India to Central Asia. The knowledge encashed in Sanskrit literature was shared even by the nomads of Central Asia. Dr. Raghu Vira, eminent scholar of world level, writes:

And the life in the *gers* and *yurts* was sanctified by the humming of *Tāntric Dharaṇis* and *Mantras* in soft melodious Sanskrit strains.[8]

Syncretism Reflected in Art

An attempt of amalgamation of Buddha and Vishnu is visible in a Buddha image with auspicious Vaishnavite symbols found in

Balawaste in the Domoko region of Xinjiang, in which Buddha's image is adorned with *shrivatsa,* diamonds, *mandara* as churning rod, horse *Uccaishrava,* the sun, the moon, *vajras,* manuscripts, triangles, and circles. The *Ucchaishrava* horse and the churning rod, in this case reminds us of the Hindu mythological story of the churning of the sea. Paintings of the Tantric type Buddhist God at Balawaste exhibit Hindu Tantric influence in Central Asia.[9]

The Shaivism was popular in Central Asia, is evident from the fact that Shiva appears on certain coins of Central Asian kings like Gondophares, Maues and many others; Shiva's images and that of the members of Shiva family — Ganesh, Kartikeya — is found on the wall paintings and wooden panels discovered in Central Asia. Professor A.M. Belenitsky, during his excavation in 1962 at Piandjikent, situated on the river Zervashan in Tajikistan, found Shiva, as represented on the fragment of a wall painting. Shiva was painted there with a circular halo and a decorated *yajñopavita,* standing in *alidha mudrā.* Clad in tiger-skin and with a trident (*trishūla*) and terrible look, Shiva has been depicted in Indian style and two attendant figures in Soghdian style. Needless to say, the artist depicting the image was accomplished in both the Indian and Soghdian traditions of Art.[10] Aurel Stein's discovery from Dandan-Uiliq in Xinjiang included a wooden panel with depiction of Shiva, about which he wrote: '...we see a three-faced and four-armed divinity, seated cross-legged on a cushion, which is supported by two couchant bulls. The flesh of the divinity is shown darkblue throughout, excepting in two side heads of which one on the right proper coloured white, bears an effeminate look, while the other is dark blue with the expression of a demon. The rich diadem of the central head with its side ornament resembling a half moon, the third eye on the forehead, the tiger-skin forming the *dhoti* or loin-cloth and finally, the bull represented as *vahana* are all so many emblems, recalling to one's mind the Brahmanic Shiva,[11] provides evidence of the prevalence of Shakta cult, along with Shaiva cult, in Central Asia. The other Hindu deities adopted in the Central Asian pantheon, and occurring on Central Asian art, are Brahmā, Indra, Ganesha, Kumāra-Kārtikeya, the Sun, the Moon and the Lokpālas.[12]

Coomaraswamy has taken notice of the Brahmā in Kucha caves of Xinjiang.[13] A figure of Indra, occurring on a fragment of a Wall painting from Balawaste, is preserved in National Museum, New

Delhi.[14] Indra's figure is identified by the eye figuring on the back of the hand. It needs mention that Indra's figures were found on some other places of Central Asia also.

Paintings of many Hindu deities — Ganesa, Kārtikeya, the Sun, the Moon, Garuda carrying nectar, and the Mahākāl — have been found in Tun-huang caves and Bezeclik. Ganesa depicted on wooden panel have been found at Dandan-Uiliq, Endere, and Khadalik also. Among the Lokapālas, the four, known as 'Caturmahārajas' — Dhritarastra, king of Gandharvas and Piśācas guarding the East; Virūdhaka, king of Kumbhandas, guarding the South; Virupāksa, king of Nāgas, guarding the West; and Vaiśravaṇa or Kubera, king of Yakṣas, guarding the North — have found place in Buddhist pantheon. These Lokapālas, considered to be warrior kings, were popular not only in Central Asia, but also in China and Japan. They have found their due place in wall paintings and sculptures of Dandan Uiliq, Kucha, Karashahr, Turfan and Rawak.

Besides the deities mentioned above, the Rama legend and the other epic stories were also known in Central Asia. Though, the *Ramayana* story differs, as we also find in South-East Asia, epic heroes — Rama, Laksamana, Sita, Dasaratha and Parasurama — used to be significantly referred; The Kharosthi documents record such epic names like Arjuna and Bhima.[15] The Krishna cult was also found to exist in Armenia in the second century B.C.[16]

Amalgamation of Buddhism and Tantric Hinduism is evident from the Buddha's figure from Balawaste, now in the Harry's collection of the National Museum, with the Tantric symbols of the sun and the moon, the two flaming jewels on lotus flowers, the two books drawn on the upper arms, also surrounded by flames and standing on lotus flowers, together with the *Vajra* on the forearms.[17] Other Tantric symbols, as B.N. Puri notes, 'include a chain ornament, a central motif alluding to life and immortality, a galloping horse and a crown alleged to be the Sassanian type symbolizing royal powers. The base has radiating lines running down from the junction with body to foot. Round the junction is apparently wrapped a snake with a part of its body protecting like a cord on each side and each part terminating in a snake's head.'[18] He further remarks that the 'whole of the device is perhaps a rendering of the churning of the ocean.'[19] In that case, the art depiction synchronizes Buddhist, Tantric and Puranic themes.

The amalgamation of Shaivism and Buddhism in Central Asia is attributed to well-known Buddhist philosopher, Asanga of about 400 A.D. Rhys Davids' opinion in this connection is worth quoting:

> 'He (Asanga) managed with great difficulty to reconcile the two opposing myths by placing a number of Saiva gods, both male and female in the inferior heavens of the prevalent Buddhism as worshippers and supporters of Buddha and Avalokiteswara. He thus made it possible for the half-converted and rude tribes to remain Buddhists while they brought offerings to their more congenial shrines and while their practical religion had no relation at all to the truths or the noble Eightfold path. They busied themselves wholly with obtaining magic phrases (*dharanis*) and magic charms.'[20]

Yet another reason of reconciliation is given by Banerjee: 'Another reason of the amalgam of Buddhism and Saivism may be due to certain factors common to them. Both Buddhism and Shaivism were originally ascetic religions and both of them were patronized largely by the merchant classes. Whatever it may be, the Shaiva pantheon held the imagination of the Central Asian people over a wide area for a long time.'[21]

Religion-wise, India and pre-Islamic Central Asia had three-way linkages through (i) Buddhism, (ii) Hinduism, and (iii) Vedism-Zoroastrianism routes. We have discussed about Buddhism in Central Asia in detail elsewhere in this book. All the communities of Central Asia — Sakas, Tusharas, Turks, Uighurs, Soghdians, Wusuns, Kangs, Mongols, etc. were Buddhists at one time or the other. Hiuen Tsang has written about Buddhist Turk kings and others in Central Asia. Many Central Asian scholars — Parthians, Kuchians/Tusharas, Khotanese and Soghdians/Kangs went to China from Central Asia and translated Sanskrit Buddhist texts from Sanskrit to Chinese.[22] Buddhist texts in Uighur, Khotanese, Tokharian, Tibetan, etc. translated from Sanskrit texts have been discovered during the excavations in Central Asia.[23] Vambery in his *History of Bukhara* writes that Turanians were idol worshippers; their king was called Pegu nezad, i.e. derived from Pegu, by which he meant 'of Buddhist origin.'[24] Of course, he also writes that the Turks residing north of Tien Shan were fire-worshippers in the seventh century A.D.[25] But both the religions were in conflict situation to each other.[26] Here, it needs mention that the worship of Fire and Sun are shared by both Zoroastrianism and Vedic religion. The very first *shukta* of *Rigveda* is in praise of *Agni* (Fire God). Vedic 'Mitra' and Zoroastrian 'Mihir' is the same. The languages of *Rigveda* and Zendavesta only phonetically differ. Therefore, Vambery rightly terms 'Zend' as 'Bactrian Pali.'[27] Moreover, *Vedas* were not unknown to the people of Central Asia. Kumarjiva learnt *Vedas*, in his return journey from Kashmir to Kucha with his mother, in Central Asia.

There are ample proof of the prevalence of Hinduism in Xinjiang[28] and western Central Asia.[29] After all the people migrating from Central Asia to India — Kushanas, Hepthals and others — remained the same, what they were there. It is a myth that they got converted to Hinduism after coming to this country. Hindu Hepthal monarch constructed Sun temple at Gwalior.[30] As reported earlier Kushanas worshipped Hindu gods. In reality, Hinduism preceded Buddhism in Central Asia.

Synchronization by Islam and Christianity

The fact needs emphasis that not only Hinduism and Buddhism worked under the overall frame of synchronization, but even the Semitic prophetic religions — Islam and Christianity — also attempted at synchronizing. Sufism was one such attempt, about which the *Dictionary of Islam* wrote that Sufism 'is but a Muslim adaptation of the *Vedanta* school of Hindu philosophers, Rabia, belonging to the second century of Islam, represented an old pagan Arab tradition. Al-Hajaj and Abu Yajid Bistami, belonging to the third century of the Islamic era, represent mainly Hindu-Buddhist tradition. The grandfather of Abu Yajid was a Zoroastrian and his teacher, Abu Ali, was from Sindh.[31] Out of four sects of Islam, Hambalis — followers of Ahmad ibn-Hambal, recognize the importance of *kayās* (opinion based on logic) and *ijmāh* (opinion of majority) also apart from Qur'an and Hadis. Ibnsaba propagated the concept of *Halul* (merger of soul in the identity of Allah). The Barmaks belonged to the family of Nav-Vihār of Bactria, which was the most famous centre of Buddhist learning in Central Asia. Abbasid Khalifas appointed Burmak prime minister; they shifted capital to Bagdad (Sanskrit, *Bhag-datta*; God gifted). It needs mention that Bagdad was established by Khalifa Mansur in 762 A.D.; it became capital in 768 A.D. Sanskrit books, especially of mathematics and medicine, were translated in Arabic. There was a more positive opening towards Persian during their regime.

Although Buddhism was rooted in the soil of Central Asia, it was the most prominent religion there; Nestorian Christianity was also quite prominent there in the seventh century A.D. Fragments of the 'New Testament' of the ninth century found in Turfan, and one of the fifth century, along with a Nestorian stone inscription are important finds in Central Asia. The inscription throws light on the doctrines and history of Nestorian Christianity it uses many Buddhist phrases. A point to be noted here is that these documents did not mention about the crucification of Christ.[32] It was under the spirit of understanding and trust that the Buddhist monks took with them the Nestorian Christian missionaries of Central Asia from Tarim basin to Ladakh to save them from the Islamic sword.[33]

Christianity was Judaic in its origin, but it became necessary for it to enter Gentile by acquiring new idiom of Gnosticism, which was the real religion, in one form or the other, of the Greco-Roman elite. The word 'gnostic' derived from 'gnosis' (Sanskrit, jñāna; knowledge, wisdom) means knowledge obtained supernaturally. The Gnostics, called 'monachos' or monks as in the *Gospel of Thomas*, lived solitary lives, sought mystical enlightenment through reflection and ascetic self-discipline. The alliance between Zudaic Christianity and Gnosticism could not last long, as both differed organizationally as well as thematically. The conflict became bitter; Gnostics were declared heretics. Christianity became the official religion in the fourth century after the conversion of Emperor Constantine; Gnostic books were banned and destroyed. In 367 A.D., Athanasius, the Archbishop of Alexandria, sent out orders for purging all apocryphal books with heretical tendencies. The Gnostic texts in an earthen jar, which were found by a peasant, Muhammad Ali in 1945 in a cliff of the Jabal al-Tarif, near Nag Hammadi, in Upper Egypt, were the ones buried by the Gnostic monks due to fear of being destroyed. These contained Coptic translations of the Greek New Testament dating back to 129-150 A.D., and some of 50-100 A.D. Elaine Pagels' *Gnostic Gospels*, brought the same to light.[34]

There are many points where there is fundamental difference

between Orthodox and Gnostic Christianity, and similarity between the latter and Hinduism. Denying the 'Otherness' of God, the Gnostics, and Vedantis also, hold that seeker and the sought are at heart one; that the self and the divine are identical; self-knowledge is the true knowledge of God. Gnostics, like the Hindus, speak not of sin and repentance but of illusion (*avidya*) and enlightenment. Hippolytus included Brahmanism as a source of Gnostic heresy. It needs insight and study in depth as to how Gnostic Christianity and Sufi Islam interacted with orthodoxy.[35]

Manichaeism and Buddhism

Manichaeism or the religion of Mani arose in Babylonia in the third century A.D. Fragments of the literature of this religion have been found in Central Asia. It is admitted that there was admixture of Buddhism in Manichaeism. As B.N. Puri has noted: 'The discoveries made in Central Asia seem to support the Chinese edict of 739 A.D. accusing Manichaeism of falsely taking the name of Buddhism and deceiving the people. This is not surprising since Mani is said to have taught, as pointed out by Al-Biruni, that Zoroaster, Buddha and Christ had preceded him as apostles and in Buddhist countries his followers naturally adopted words and symbols familiar to the people.'[36]

Puri further writes: 'Thus, Manichaean deities are represented like Bodhisattvas sitting cross-legged on a lotus. Mani receives the epithet Ju-lai or Tathagat as in Amida's Paradise. There are holy trees bearing flowers which enclose beings styled Buddha, and the construction and phraseology of Manichaean books resemble those of a Buddhist Sutra.'[37]

Manichaeans accepted the Bodhisattva Kṣitigarbha as one of the 'Envoys of light'. This suggests impact or action of Buddhism on Manichaenism. In popularity, he is equal to Bodhisattva Avalokiteśvara in the Far East.[38] Although, development of Kṣitigarbha's cult was a regional phenomenon, its spiritual content and overall framework remained under Buddhism. In this case, it needs to be remembered that the cultural and spiritual soil of Central Asia was fertile enough to produce a Manjuśri — he was Tokharian in birth—, a Kṣitigarbha, and a towering scholar like Kumārajiva.

To conclude, it needs mention that there was constant movement of men and ideas within India, Central Asia and Iran; many of their gods were common; their Sun God (Veda, *Mitra*; Avestā, *Mihira*) travelled even up to the far west corner of Europe. The spiritual tradition, unlike the Semitic one, was open, and conducive for the cult syncretism.

References

1. *Numismatic Chronicle,* 1893, pp. 126-127, pl. X, fig. 2.
2. Banerjee, P., *Hindu Deities in Central Asia,* in Lokesh Chandra *et al.* (Ed.) *India's Contribution to World Thought and Culture,* Madras (1970), p. 282; he refers *Cf.* Les Chionites, Hepthalites, pp. 55-58, Fig. 65 and Pl. vii, I; J.N. Banerjee, *The Development of Hindu Iconography,* pp. 124-25.
3. Litvinsky, B.A.; *Outline of History of Buddhism in Central Asia,* p.8; International Conference of the History, Archaeology, and Culture of Central Asia in the Kushan Period, Dushanbe.
4. Majumdar, R.C.; *Suvarnadvipa: Ancient Indian Colonies in the Far East,* Vol. 2; (Reprint); New Delhi, 1986; p. 106; He brings to reference Dr. Goris, *History of the Indian Archipelago,* Vol. II, p. 207.
5. *Ṛgveda* I.164.46.
6. *Ibid.*
7. *Ṛgveda,* 9.58.2; translated by Professor Raghu Vira.
8. Dr. Raghu Vira, in *India and Central Asia: A Cultural Symphony.*
9. Banerjee, *op. cit.*, p. 272. Stein found similar painting at Dandan-Uiliq. (Stein, *Ancient Khotan,* Pl. XL.
10. Banerjee, *op. cit.*, p. 284; he refers, *Śiva Icon from Piandjikent,* by the author; *Artibus Asiae,* Vol. XXXI, 1969.
11. Stein, *Ancient Khotan,* Vol. I, p. 261, Pl. LXII. The *Trimurti Śiva* finds in Xinjiang, kept in National Museum, New Delhi.
12. Banerjee, *op. cit.*, p. 285.
13. Banerjee, *op. cit.*; Coomaraswamy, *History of Indian and Indonesian Art,* London, 1927, p. 150 notes.
14. Banerjee, *op. cit.*, p. 285; *Catalogue of Wall-Paintings from Ancient Shrines in Central Asia and Sistan,* p. 13.
15. Professor Bailey, *"Tha Rama Story in Khotanese", Journal of the American Oriental Society,* JAOS, LIX, pp. 460-68.
16. *Journal of the Royal Asiatic Society of Great Britain and Ireland,* 1904; pp. 310ff.
17. Puri, B.N.; *Buddhism in Central Asia*; Reprint, Delhi (2000); pp. 270-71.
18. *Ibid.*, p. 271.

19. *Ibid.*
20. Rhys Davids, *Buddhism*, London (1877), p. 208; referred by Banerjee, *op. cit.*, p. 283.
21. Banerjee, *op. cit.*, p. 283.
22. For detailed information, read *Buddhism in Central Asia*, by B.N. Puri, and *Madhya Asia ka Itihas* (Hindi) by Rahul Sankrityayan.
23. Puri, *op. cit.*, pp. 23, 23n, 181n, 214; 206; 213; 62; 223, etc.
24. Vambery, Arminius; *History of Bukhara*, London (1873), p. 14.
25. *Ibid.*, p. 13 note.
26. *Ibid.*, p. 14.
27. *Ibid.*, p. 7
28. Sankrityayan, *op. cit.*, pp. 203-04.
29. Gupta, S.P.; *Hindu Gods in Western Central Asia*, in *India and Central Asia: Classical to Contemporary Period*, J.N. Roy and B.B. Kumar (Ed.), New Delhi, pp. 57-62. Dialogue, Vol. 3, No. 2; New Delhi (2002), pp. 142-46.
30. Sankrityayan, *op. cit.*, p. 222.
31. Ram Swarup, *Hindu View of Christianity and Islam*, pp. 98-99.
32. Puri, *op. cit.*, pp. 139-40.
33. Sankrityayan, *op. cit.*, p. 143.
34. Ram Swarup, *Hinduism and Monotheistic Religions*, pp. 337-345.
35. *Ibid.*
36. Puri, *op. cit.*, pp. 136-139.
37. *Ibid.*
38. *Ibid.*, pp. 146, 337; Eliot, *Hinduism and Buddhism*, p. 221.

8

Brahmi, Kharosthi and Other Scripts of Indian Origin

The use of Brahmi (*Brāhmī*) and Kharosthi (*Kharoṣṭhi*) scripts were prevalent in Central Asia since early days. Numerous manuscripts of various languages, including Sanskrit, Prakrit — Niya/Gandhari Prakrit in Tarim basin, i.e., Xinjiang, and Sogdian Prakrit or *Cūlikā Paiśāchi* Prakrit in Samarkand, Balkh, Khorezm and Merv areas of Western Turkistan — and other languages, of the books and their fragments and the documents of secular nature, written in these scripts have been discovered from a vast area of Central Asia from Tun-huwang in the east to Merv, in Turkmenistan, in the west. While Brahmi was used for writing Sanskrit almost everywhere in Central Asia, the script was also used for writing the languages of Kucha or Kuchi (Kuchean), Karasahr (ancient Agnideśa; the language called Agnean) and Khotan (Saka-Khotanese) in the Tarim basin. It was also used sometimes with other scripts on the same leaves of manuscripts. In some manuscript sheets from Khara-Khota, Turfan and Majar Taqh, Brahmi is used along with Chinese or Uighur. In a manuscript containing a Buddhist Chinese text written in Brahmi script, similar to those used in Saka-Khotanese documents, the relationship of the Brahmi script with the Chinese language is traced.[1]

The use of Brahmi script, and its association with Buddhism, preceded that of Kharosthi, at least in the cities of northern route of Xinjiang, i.e. Kucha and Karasahr. In Khotan region, however, Brahmi script was a late-comer. In western Turkistan, Brahmi inscriptions — donative and didactive — have been found at Kara Tepe. Ashvaghosha's (Aśvaghoṣa's) dramas in Brahmi script were discovered from Turfan region. This manuscript, written in purely Indian variety script of the time of the Kushanas and the Guptas, is placed in about the middle of the second century A.D. on palaeographic ground. Needless to say that the fragments of the Aśvaghoṣa's dramas were among the earliest Sanskrit manuscripts in Brahmi script. The whole text of the *Pratitya-samutpāda-sūtra* discovered from Tun-huang area is also in the early Brahmi script. A manuscript containing fragments of the Kumaralāta's *Kalpanāmaṇḍitikā*, believed to be of the first half of the fourth century A.D., was written in Gupta script. The well-known Bower manuscripts are also of the fourth or fifth century AD.[2]

Apart from the earliest Brahmi script used for writing Sanskrit in Central Asia, there were two other distinct script varieties, derived from the old Brahmi script, known as the 'slanting' Gupta script and the 'upright' Gupta script. In Central Asia, Agnean, Kuchean and Khotanese used slanting Gupta script; even the Chinese in the region used cursive Gupta characters. This is, of course, apart from *Siddha-mātrikā* script of Indian origin, which is prevalent throughout China, Korea and Japan; many Tibetan language manuscripts have been found in Central Asia, especially in Tun-huang. The Tibetan script, it needs mention, was invented by Saṁbhoṭa, the Minister of the King who founded the state of Tibet and established the capital of Lhasa in 639 A.D. The Tibetan script spread up to the borders of Mongolia; it was adopted by such languages as Man, and even Chinese has been written in the same.[3]

As mentioned above, both 'slanting' and 'upright' Gupta scripts— both derived from Brahmi — were in use in Central Asia. Northern or Kuchean Brahmi script, noted for its upright ductus, according to Hoernle, was imported from India through immigrants,[4] and in it developed a more or less starting ductus at the hands of the locals. As some of the fragments of the manuscripts discovered in the northern area of Kucha shows true upright Gupta of the fourth or fifth century, along with the slanting type, it is believed that the latter must have developed at a very early period.[5]

Brahmi script was a late-comer in Khotan or southern Xinjiang than the same in northern region. Earlier documents found in the Khotan and Shan-Shan, etc. have been written in Kharosthi script.[6] But the sporadic use of the Brahmi in southern Xinjiang in early centuries of the Christian era was also traced, in which, there were three lines in Brahmi script of the Kusana period recorded on a wooden tablet with a Kharosthi inscription on the other side.[7] A mutilated folio and a fragment of a Palm-leaf *pothi* in Sanskrit from

Miran, written in the upright Brahmi script of the early Gupta age (no. M.11.0011) were also found. These documents, including a *pothi,* seeming to be a part of a grammatical work, were dated to *c.* A.D., 400 by Hoernle.[8] In as late as in sixth/seventh centuries, Brahmi seems to be popular in Khotan as per the testimony of Chinese travellers, Sung-yun and Hsuan-tsang. Saka — including Khotanese — manuscripts written in Brahmi, datable between seventh and tenth centuries A.D. have been found in Khotan region. The manuscripts written in slanting Gupta script have, however, not come to light in Khotan region.[9]

There is mention of a script called *Khāsyalipi* in *Lalitavistara* (supposed to be of second or third century A.D.); Ptolemy calls it *Khāsāozi.* Kashgar, strategically located on the eastern slopes of Pamir in Tarim basin — also identified as Yangi-Hissar — is linked to Khasya or Khasa people.[10] It needs mentioning that Khasas, spread from Central Asia to Kashmir and western Nepal, were well-known to the Indians. They were ethnically, linguistically and religiously linked to India. Most probably, Khasyalipi must have linkages either to Brahmi or Kharosthi.

Kharosthi script was used in Central Asia for writing Prakrit language. Huge collection of manuscripts written in Kharosthi have been discovered in Central Asia and studied. The script is found also in the Sino-Kharosthi coins in the region.[11] The earliest use of Kharosthi script, as suggested by a Kharosthi record from Tajikistan, takes us back to first century A.D.[12] The script was also used for writing Prakrit in North-Western India, especially in the Gandhar region. Because of the linguistic similarity, Niya Prakrit of Central Asia is also called Gandhari Prakrit. Kharoshti, as we know is also an Indian script; it is written from right to left as against Brahmi, which is written from left to right.

The British colonial writers — Thomas, Cunningham and Taylor — claimed that Kharosthi script was derived from Aramic.[13] Euro-centrism and Middle-East centrism have been the dominant trend of colonial and church-related scholarship in India. They invented many myths and lies while writing about Indian history and culture. The opinion of the colonial trio should be taken in that light only. Here, it needs mention that even name of that script is Indian. The very name of the script 'Kharosthi' is a Sanskrit term. It means 'lip of an ass' (*khara,* Sanskrit = ass; *ostra, oṣṭha* = lip). The shape of the letters might have been the cause of such nomenclature. The script follows Indian phonetic system; there is separation of vowels and consonants; letters of alphabet are arranged according to the Indian phonetic system of separation of vowels and consonants; the framework is of *Pratisakhya/siksas.* Evidently, the script cannot be of any foreign origin.

References

1. Stein, Aurel; *Innermost Asia,* Vol. III, Pl. cxxv; *Serindia,* Pl. cii.; B.N. Puri, *Buddhism in Central Asia,* p. 187.
2. Mookerji, B.N., p. 707; Bagchi, P.C., *India and Central Asia,* p. 93; Puri, *op. cit.*, p. 186.
3. Prof. Dr. Raghu Vira, *India and Asia—A Cultural Symphony,* New Delhi, 1978, pp. 17-18.
4. Hoernle, Rudolf, *Manuscript Remains of Buddhist Literature found in Eastern Turkistan,* London, 1916; p. xiii.
5. Hoernle, *op. cit.*, p. xiii, n. 14; quoted by B.N. Puri, *Buddhism in Central Asia,* p. 186.
6. Bagchi, *op. cit.*, p. 93.
7. Stein, *Ancient Khotan,* Vol. I, Oxford, 1907, p. 369; Puri, *op. cit.*, p. 187 note 32; *The Cultural Heritage of India,* p.709
8. Stein, *Serindia,* p. 489.
9. Puri, *op. cit.*, p. 187, 32 n.
10. *Ibid.*, p. 106.
11. Agrawala, *Some Aspects of Indian Culture in the Kharosthi Documents from Chinese Turkistan.* In India's Contribution to World Thought and Culture, Lokesh Chandra; p. 275.
12. *Ibid.*, p. 187 note 32.
13. *The Cultural Heritage of India,* Calcutta, Reprint, 1991; p. 228.

9

Manuscript Finds in Central Asia

Explorations and excavations by various missions sent by different nationalities in Central Asia, especially Eastern Turkistan, resulted in huge manuscript finds, mostly in Sanskrit and Prakrit languages, but also in Kuchean, Khotanese, Sogdian, Uighur, Chinese, Tibetan and Syriac languages. The subject matter of the Sanskrit manuscripts and the fragments of Sanskrit texts, and their translations, mostly concerned Buddhism of the Sarvastivadin and Mahasanghika (Mahayana) schools; the latter ones were found to be in the more evolved esoteric forms. The script used for Sanskrit texts was Brahmi. Prakrit texts, mostly of secular nature, used Kharosthi. Imported palm leaves, birch bark, wood or bamboo plates, leather and paper were used as the printing materials.

Regular campaigns for the collection of manuscripts by government representatives, as well as private parties, started in the last quarter of the nineteenth century. Agents were also employed for the purpose. The remains of ancient civilization were discovered by a Russian Archaeological Mission from Idikutshahri, Qocho, Quarakhojo, Turfan and Murtuk in the Turfan oasis of northern Xinjiang. After chance-discoveries of Sanskrit manuscripts by Bower and Prakrit *Dhammapada* in Kharosthi script by French traveller Dutreuil de Rhins, the interest of Government of India was aroused. Aurel Stein, a trained Archaeologist in the Government service and thoroughly acquainted with the routes of North-West frontier was deputed for archaeological explorations in the region of Khotan. The findings were published in Stein's book *Ancient Khotan*. Three German missions, under Grunwedel and Von Lecoq between 1903 and 1907, followed. There were altogether four German expeditions. A. Regal, a German botanist in the service of Russia, went on the expedition in the oasis of Turfan earlier in northern Xinjiang in 1879.

The French expedition, under the leadership of famous Sinologist Paul Pelliot, was sent in 1906. Palliot carried out the investigations from 1906 to 1908 in northern part of Xinjiang in Tumshuk, Kucha and Kizil; passed most part of his time in studying manuscript collections and the art remains of the Tunhuang Caves of Thousand Buddhas. Russia sent two missions in 1906 and 1908 under the leadership of Beresovsky and Kazaloff. Japanese missions were sent under Count Otani in 1904, and another under Tachibana a few years later. Government of India sent Stein again in 1906 and then in 1913 for investigations in Central Asia.[1]

Stein, during his second exploratory mission during 1906-08, covered the ancient sites of Domoko, Niya, Lou-lan, and Miran beyond Khotan on the southern route. The findings of his explorations have been detailed in the volumes of *Ser-India.* Stein covered a very wide 'area, including Khotan, Niya, Lou-lan, Tunhuang, Borkul, Guchen, Jimasa, Idikutshahri Kucha and Aksu during his third expedition during 1913-16. The records of his third exploration are detailed in his *Inner Asia.*[2]

The expedition of Col. Bower in 1891 resulted in the acquisition of famous birch bark codex manuscripts, called Bower manuscripts, preserved in the Bodlein library at Oxford. Out of the seven texts, said to be of fourth century A.D.[3], three had medical texts. In reality, Bower was sent by Government of India on a confidential mission in search of a murderer and a man of Kucha took him to a subterranean town to dig treasures. While digging, he found the oldest Sanskrit manuscripts of that time. The medical texts, which Bower discovered by chance were three Ayurvedic texts, namely, *Navanitaka,* (cream) *Pasaka-kevali* and *Mahāmāyuri. Navanitaka* contained an abstract of the earlier medical literature, including those of Agnidesa, Bheda, Jatikarṇa, Kṣarapāṇi, Parāśara and Suśruta. Several manuscripts of even earlier period were discovered after that, such as the dramatic fragments of Aśvaghoṣa, collected by the German mission, and the manuscript of the *Udānavarga* by the French mission. Both written in quasi-Kusana character of the second century, were important acquisitions. It needs mention that the *Udānavarga* was the Sanskrit version of the *Dhammapada.* Dutrevil de Rhines and Grenard of the 1892 French Mission discovered the birch-bark manuscript of *Prakrit Dhammapada* near Khotan. The great Hungarian explorer Aurel Stein led several

Indian missions, discovered large number of Kharosthi Prakrit documents along with other manuscript finds and paintings near Niya and Tun-huang. Stein, Dutrevil de Rhine and A. Von Le Cog of the German mission did pioneering work in the field of exploration and excavation in the Xinjiang. J.K. Dabbs and Kali Das Nag provided information about these discoveries in their books.[4] Rudolf Hoernle has catalogued the British collection in his *Manuscript Remains of Buddhist Literature found in Eastern Turkistan.*

The four German expeditions to Eastern Turkistan, between 1903 and 1964, brought back to Berlin the Sanskrit manuscripts forming major part of the Turfan collection of the manuscripts and block prints. More than 7,000 catalogue numbers of the Sanskrit manuscripts have already been allocated and parts 1 to 9 of the catalogue series, titled *Sanskrithandschriften aus den Turfan funded* (abbreviated SHT), have been described and catalogued as a part of *Union Catalogue of Oriental Manuscripts in German Collections* by June 2005.[5] Apart from the finds from sites, such as Tumsuq, Qizil, etc. in Kucha region, and Xoco, Murtuq/Beezeklik, Toyoq, etc. in Turfan oasis; some manuscripts were also acquired from the market. Soon after the return of the first expedition in 1903, the first Sanskrit texts were published. Richard Pischel, who held chair of Indology in Berlin University at that time, edited fragments of three block prints — two of which identified later on as belonging to the *Samyuktāgam* — and published the same in two volumes. Two publications by Heinrich Stonner, working then in the Museum of Ethnology in Berlin, included the short *Dharmaśarirasūtra* and three folios of a block print of the *Suvarṇabhāsottamasūtra.* Three other publications during 1907 and 1908 included fragments of a Sanskrit grammar by Emil Sieg and first fragments of the *Udānvarga* by Pischel. Heinrich Luders, who succeeded Pischel after his early death in 1908, and Luders' wife Else continued the work afterwards. Luder's edition of *Bruchstucke Buddhistischer Dramen* was published as first part of the series "Kleinere Sanskrit-Texte" in 1911. Luders, around 1912, started scientific processing of Sanskrit texts from Turfan, and Sanskrit texts from Khotan sent by A.F.R. Hoernle from London. He processed four folios of the Kashgar manuscript of the *Saddharmapuṇḍarīkasūtra,* one folio of another manuscript of the same, and fragment of yet another folio, identified recently by Jin-il Chung as a *sūtra* of the *Madhyamāgama.* These manuscripts were published in Hoernle's *Manuscript Remains of Buddhist Literature Found in Eastern Turkistan* in 1916. The work of editing and publication of Sanskrit books, interrupted due to First World War, started in Berlin again only in 1922. Else Luders for more than twenty years laboriously performed the work of transliteration, of countless fragments, reuniting matching parts of manuscripts and identification of several fragments, possibly with the help of her husband, Heinrich Luders. Elsa Luders, for the first time, arranged the manuscripts according to their contents for different genres. Many manuscripts were lost during Second World War, although some of the lost ones were recovered later on. In such cases, the researchers were immensely helped, as they used the transliterated copies of the original manuscripts. Thus, it is clear that Elsa's work was immensely useful, although she never edited any manuscript.

The Turfan Sanskrit manuscripts were removed from Berlin and shifted to Gottingen in 1943 to avoid them from destruction from the air raids; these were brought back to Berlin again only in 1947. During transport from Berlin to Gottingen, two-thirds of the glass plates were cracked and a few had lost their labels with numbers. They were arranged and remounted between sheets of glass again. The same thing happened when the manuscripts were brought back to Berlin. Emil Sieg, heading chair of Indology in Gottingen, his successor and Luder's pupil, Ear Waldschmidt, and Waldschmidt's pupils — Herbert Hartel, Kusum Mittal, Valentina Rosen, Dieter Schlingloff, Chandrabhal Tripathi and some others played most important roles in scientific processing, editing and cataloguing of the manuscripts. When about 1000 glass plates supposed to be Tokharian texts were sent to Emil Sieg, it was found that the same were Sanskrit texts and Waldschmidt had already worked on in some cases in Berlin. Waldschmidt did his doctorate under Heinrich Luders with edition of *Bhikṣuṇīpratimokṣa* from the Turfan collections; his post-doctoral thesis from 1930 and again edition of Manuscript fragment, was from a collection of Buddhist *sūtras.* He remained associated with the Oriental Commission, and then with the newly founded 'Institute of Oriental Research of the German Academy of Sciences in Berlin, which pioneered the work. Waldschmidt and his co-workers worked at Gottingen to provide a provisional catalogue of the Turfan finds basing on the transliterations of Else Luders and photo copies of the Sanskrit manuscripts made available in Gottingen.

The work of cataloguing of Turfan texts continued for decades; from catalogue number SHT part 1 to SHT part 9 have been published between 1965 to 2004. Three more volumes were planned up to 2015. Thus all the Sanskrit manuscripts of the Turfan finds will be described by then. Apart from the SHT volumes, three major text editions also came out during last few years, namely Matṛceṭa's *Varṇarnāha-varṇanāstotra* by J.U. Hartmann, the *Pratimokṣasūtra* in two volumes by Georg von Simson, and an unknown *Abhidharma* text; the last one is also the so-called Spitzer Manuscript, by Eli Franco. The first two editions also include the relevant manuscript fragments collected in London, Paris and St. Petersburg. The SHT work has generated worldwide interest in the Sanskrit manuscript collections, which interest not only the Sanskrit scholars but also the scholars working in other fields. The collection includes several glosses in Tocharian and Uigur also. The scholars' interest in SHT publications is evident from the fact that there is constant flow of communication from the readers about the identifications and suggestions about the manuscripts, which get included in the addenda of the SHT Part 4 onwards. Again, 171 publications came out, as reported sometime back, which were based on these publications.[6]

British Library, in its Hoernle and Stein collections, has the Sanskrit manuscript fragments consisting of more than 4,500 items. The manuscripts were studied and edited by comparing them with their Chinese and Tibetan versions by the distinguished Japanese scholars of Soka University, Tokyo. The edited matter has been published in the book, *The British Library Sanskrit Fragments*, Vols. I, II.1 and II.2, Soka University, Tokyo. A fragment of *Sukhāvati vyūha* on the Silk Route was discovered by a Japanese; it was the only copy found outside Japan. Aurel Stein dug a manuscript of *Vajracchedicā* from the ruins of a small dwelling place in Dandan Uiliq; F.E. Pargiter dated it to fifth century AD.[7]

As manuscript finds during Cental Asian explorations reveal, Sanskrit Tripiṭaka was the canon of the Sarvāstivāda School, it consisted of *Sūtrapiṭaka; Vinayapiṭaka* and *Abhidharmapiṭaka.* Whereas Sanskrit *Sūtrapiṭaka* was the collection of four *Āgamas*, Pali *Sūtrapiṭaka* had five *Nikāyas.* The manuscripts of the *Saṅgiti-Sūtra* and *Aṭanāṭiya-Sūtra* of *Dirghāgama*, the *Upāli-Sūtra* and *Śuka-Sūtra* of the *Madhyamāgama*, and the *Pravaraṇa-Sūtra, Candropama-Sūtra, Śakti-Sūtra, Nidāna-Sūtra, Kokanada-Sūtra, Anāthapiṇḍaka-Sūtra, Dīrghanakha-Sūtra, Sarabha-Sūtra, Parivrājaka-sthavira-Sūtra* and *Brāhmaṇa-Satyāṁsu-Sūtra* of the *Saṁyuktāgama* have been discovered from Central Asia. Complete text of the *Pratimokṣa-sūtra* and portions of *Bhikṣuṇī-Pratimokṣa* (both collected from Kucha region) and some other fragments of *Vinaya Piṭaka* were also found. The discovery included fragment texts of the *Abhidharma Piṭaka* also. Manuscripts finds of *Mūlasarvāstivāda Vinaya* from Turfan region included *Civara-vastu, Karmavācana* and *Vinaya-vibhanga.* Mahayana texts discovered in the region included *Vajracchedikā, Ratnasari-Sūtra, Ratnadhvaja-Sūtra, Candragarbha-Sūtra, Candrapāla-Sūtra, Mahāparinirvāṇa-Sūtra, Saddharma-puṇḍarika-Sūtra, Dasabhumika-Sūtra, Dharmaśarira-Sūtra, Gaṇḍavyūha-Sūtra, Satasahasrikā Prajñāpāramitā, Suvarṇaprabhāsa-Sūtra,* and *Samādhirāja-Sūtra.* The finds of *dhāraṇis,* i.e. magical formula of later Mahayana, were *Mahāmāyurī-vidyārajñi, Ananta-mukha-dhāraṇī, Surāngaṁa-samādhī, Sitatapatradhāraṇī, Mahapratyangira-dhāraṇī,* and *Vajrapāṇi-sumukhanāma-dhāraṇī.* The discovery of these manuscripts brought to light the fact that Mahayana canon was also studied in Central Asia. One knew about these books only through their Chinese, Tibetan, Khotanese, Kuchean, Yuighur translation.[8] The dramas of Aśvaghoṣa and many other books also came to light for the first time, as their originals were lost.

Apart from the canonical texts, a large number of non-canonical texts in Sanskrit were also discovered in the region. Fragments of three Sanskrit dramas of Aśvaghoṣa written in Kusaṇa Brāhmi characters on palm-leaf were found in Kucha area of Tarim basin; one of which was *Sāriputra-prakaraṇa.* One of the remaining two deals with a theme concerning courtesans; the third one is an allegorical drama with dialogues among three characters, namely *Buddhi* (wisdom or prudence), *Dhṛti* (steadfastness) and *Kirtti* (fame). These manuscripts supposedly belonged to Kaniska's period. Another manuscript of a later date of *Sāriputra-prakaraṇa* was also discovered from the Kucha area. The copy of the same has not yet been found anywhere outside Central Asia. Again, two manuscripts of Aśvaghoṣa's dramas — *Buddha-carita* and *Saundarānanda-kāvya* — were recovered from the ruins of

Shorchuq.[9] Manuscripts of a poetical work in Sanskrit, titled *Kalpanā-maṇḍitikā* or *Kalpanā-maṇḍitikā-dṛṣṭantapaṅkti* were recovered from Kucha and Turfan; the author's name given therein was Kumarlāta. It agrees with the Chinese translation of Asvaghosa's Sutrālalaṁkāra done by Kumarajiva in the early fifth century. In H. Luders' opinion, Chinese version was wrongly attributed to Kumarajiva; in reality, it was the work of Kumaralāta, a famous Buddhist scholar of Sautrāntika School and founder of the Dārstantika branch.[10]

A large number of the Sanskrit manuscripts of the hymns have been recovered from Tumshuq, Kucha, Shorchuq, Turfan and Tunhuang. Some of them are *Śatapañcaśatica-Stotra, Anaparaddha-stotra* and *Varṇārha-varṇa-stotra* (*Varṇārha-varṇa Buddhastotra Catuḥśatakam*). These poetic works and many others recovered from Tarim basin region are attributed to Matriceta, supposed to be a contemporary of Asvaghosa. Other manuscript finds of the region include Āryasura's *Jātakamālā, Chandoviciti,* a work on metrics, *Katāntra,* a grammatical work. The *Jātakamālā* is preserved in a Khotanese metrical translation done by Vidyāśīla in the Samanya monastery in the second half of the tenth century A.D.[11]

A large number of'Manuscript finds in Eastern Turkistan have been written in Kharosthi script, the language of the same is Prakrit, labelled as Niya Prakrit, as well as, Gandhari Prakrit. The Prakrit language documents are usually known as Kharosthi documents. We have discussed about the same separately.

Considerable literary remains in the languages of the settlements of the northern and southern routes of Tarim basin, mostly the translations of the canonical and non-canonical texts, have also been discovered by different excavation missions. Most of the Kuchean manuscripts were, however, collected by the French Mission, and only few were from the Stein, Russian and German collections. Sylvain Levy, and later on Jean Filliozat, studied the French, Russian and Stein's collections and published their findings. The German Mission discovered 417 fragments of texts in Karasahr and Turfan regions, which were edited by Sieg and Siegling and were published with plates in the volume titled *Tocharische, Sprachreste.* The fact has come to light that Kuchean, rather than the Tocharian was the language of the common man, in which the mural inscriptions in the Buddhist caves of the area were written. Tocharian books were written elsewhere and brought in the region.

It, however, needs mention that the manuscripts mentioned were translated from Sanskrit, and some of them, such as, *Pratimokṣa, Prāyaṣchittikā* and *Pratideśaniya* of *Sarvāstivāda-Vinaya*, are bilingual with original Sanskrit by the side of translations. These texts must have been prepared for monks understanding less Sanskrit or as handbooks for teaching Sanskrit. Apart from bilingual manuscripts, others included translations of *Udānavarga, Udānastotra* and *Udānālaṁkāra.* Kuchean translations of a very extensive Sanskrit text, *Karmavibhaṅga,* dealing with the retribution of acts (*karma*) and the doctrine of transmigration, and a medical text *Yogasataka* were also found.[12]

Fragments of translations of the Buddhist texts have also been found. Some of such works, e.g, *Udanavarga,* is bilingual. Khotanese texts, generally of the late period when Hinayana disappeared from Khotan, include the translations of *Suvarṇaprabhāsa-Sūtra, Vajracchedikā, Aparimitāyuṣa-Sūtra, Bhadrācāryādeśanā, Jātakāstava* and *Maitreya-Samiti-nāṭaka.* Khotanese finds of the manuscripts include translations of two Indian medical texts, namely *Siddhasāra,* written by one Ravigupta, and *Jivakapustaka.* The Khotanese rendering was based on Tibetan translation; may be Sanskrit original was lost. The original *Jivakapustaka* is not found. But interlinear Sanskrit verses show that the book was originally written in Sanskrit.[13]

The Central Asian manuscript finds also include Sogdian and Turkish translations of certain Buddhis texts. The Sogdian manuscripts include *Dirghanakha-Sūtra, Vessāntara-Jātaka, Vimalakīrti-Nirdeśa, Dhyānsūtra, Dhutasūtra, Nilakaṇṭha-dhāraṇī* and *Padmacintāmaṇī-dhāraṇī-Sūtra.* In Turkish, the manuscripts include *Maitreyasamiti-nāṭaka, Suvarṇaprabhāṣa-Sūtra, Jātakas, Sūtra of Kalyāṇaṁkāra* and *Papaṁkāra,* etc. A few Brahmi documents were no doubt found in Turkish; but the knowledge of Sanskrit became almost obsolete.[14]

The manuscript finds in Central Asia confirmed Indian linkages with Central Asia sinçe deep antiquity, revealed the fact that the region had ruling dynasties of Indian origin, had Indian way of life and belief—system, used Indian languages — Sanskrit and Prakrit — and Indian scripts — Brahmi and Kharosthi. The use of Sanskrit for Buddhist literature was also a revealation.

References

1. Bagchi, Prabodh Chandra; *India and Central Asia,* Calcutta, 1955; pp. 90-91.
2. *Ibid.*, p. 91.
3. *Journal of the Asiatic Society of Bengal* (*JASB*), 1891, pp. 79ff.
4. *History of the Discovery and Exploration of Chinese Turkistan,* J.K. Dabbs; London (1971); *Greater India,* Kali Das Nag; Bombay (1969).
5. Klaus Wille in his *Survey of the Sanskrit Manuscripts in the Turfan Collection* informs briefly about the work of editing and publication of Sanskrit manuscripts found in Xinjiang.
6. *Ibid.*
7. Lokesh Chandra, 'Sanskrit in the Silk Route', *Dialogue,* Vol. 15, No. 3.
8. The *Cultural Heritage of India,* pp. 711-12; P.C. Bagchi, *op. cit.*, pp. 94ff; *Journal of Asiatic Society,* Vol. XI, pp. 63ff;
9. Bagchi, P.C.; *op. cit.*, pp. 100-101.
10. The Cultural Heritage of India, p. 713.
11. *Ibid.*, p. 714; P.C., Bagchi, *op. cit.*, pp. 101-102; B.N. Puri, *Buddhism in Central Asia,* p. 207.
12. Bagchi, *op. cit.*, pp. 105-106; *Cultural Heritage of India,* pp. 715-18.
13. *Ibid.*, p. 107.
14. *Ibid.*, pp. 108-11.

10

Kharosthi Documents in Xinjiang

Sir Aurel Stein discovered 764 documents written on wood boards (*takhtis*), silk, leather and paper in the Kharosthi (*Kharoṣṭhī*) script, called Kharosthi documents, from Niya, Endere and Loulan of Xinjiang in around 1900 AD. T. Burrow edited another 18 Kharosthi documents after that, raising the total number of the same to 782.[1] Not only the script, but even the language Prakrit (*Prākṛta*), named Niya Prakrit, of the documents was an Indian one. Being similar to the Prakrit spoken in the Gandhar region of the North-West India, the language is also termed as the Gandhari Prakrit. These documents, mostly of a secular nature containing royal messages, personal letters, court deeds and state archival materials, provide valuable information about Indian way of life during early centuries of Christian era in the heart of Central Asia.[2]

Kharosthi documents throw enough light on family and social life, material culture, land and agriculture, professions, food and drinks, clothes and garments, languages, religion, social ethos, political life, etc. in Xinjiang. The terms, used in the documents, are mostly Prakrit, derived from Sanskrit.

Family and Social Life

The family, as depicted in the documents, consisted of the father, mother, brothers and young sisters (nos. 164, 195); the headman exercised authority over them (nos. 450, 562).[3] The terms used, mostly Indian, for father (*pitā, pitu*), mother (*mātu, mādu,* etc.), brother (*bhrāta, bhrātu*), sister (*svasu,* Sanskrit – *Svaśru*), son (*putra, suta*), daughter (*putri, dhitū*), wife (*bhāryā*), grandfather (*pitūmaha*; Sanskrit, *Pitamaha*), grandson (*prapotra, praoutra*; Sanskrit, *Pautra*), son-in-law (*jāmāta*), brother's son (*bhrāta-putra*), nāpata [daughter's (son), family (*parivāra*)], dynasty (*kula*), etc. were either Sanskrit or Prakrit ones. *Visatitaga* (Sanskrit — viśa) in a particular inscription also denotes family. The terms *kuda* and *kudi* for male and female child respectively have currency in Punjabi language also. The terms used for the male slave (Sanskrit — *dāsa*) was *dāsa, dajha, dhajha, dajhajamna,* and the same for female slave (Sanskrit, *dāsī*) was *dāsī, dajhi*; the slave-owner or master was *bhatāra* (Sanskrit, *bhattāraka*).[4]

New members were added to the family by adoption and purchase of slaves, as even slaves were treated as family members. Both boys and girls (nos. 331, 542, etc.), and even elderly ladies (528) were adopted after payment after proper consideration (*kutichhara*) in cash or in kind. (11, 31).[5]

The birth of a son used to be an occasion of great rejoicing and happiness, as mentioned in document number 702: *putra-jāta, savehṛ sātenabhavitavya.* But the birth of a daughter was not viewed with disfavour. The expression "*satayupramanas*", in a letter of a son to his father, reminds us of the general life expectancy of a hundred years in India (*jiveṁ saradaḥ sataṁ, srinuyāṁ saradaḥ sataṁ*; may we live for hundred years, may we hear for hundred years). The long epithet used by the son for his father in that letter is worth-quoting, which is: "*priyadarsanas deva-manus-saṃpūjitus pichara divyavarṣa-śatāyupramānasa priyapitu*". The document number 511 states that 'all creatures, on entering the doctrine of Tathagatas, make end of birth and death'. Leading noble and chaste life is emphasized in document number 399 (*samprajya Kartavya, kujala kartavya, brahmacharita*). Several documents remind the king to abide by the law (*dharma*); the epithet used for a king in several documents is *sachadhamastidasa.* Needless to say that the society, depicted in the documents, was dominated by Hindu-Buddhist thought, culture and ethos.[6]

The documents include numerous letters written to near and dear ones, such as, a letter affectionately written by a monk to his brother (no. 646), two letters written to friends in sincere and well-wishing tone (*kalyāṇakārī*; nos. 499, 612), a lady addressing her sister as a pleasing personality (*priyadarśinī*) and pointing to literacy among upper strata of the society (no. 316), letters conveying good and bad news to the daughter and son-in-law (690), wife's brother (*syālā;* nos. 140 and 475), etc.[7]

There is a mention about the sale and purchase of girls in and around Niya in Xinjiang, which, "was in no way an Indian practice."

An author writes: "The society was mixed, containing not only the Hindus from India but also the locally born people".[8] It seems that the author forgets that even India did not have uniform tradition in such case, and confuses the payment of bride-price, so common even among numerous castes and tribes of India, for the sale and purchase of girls. Many communities in India, has even the tradition of the returning back of the bride-price in case there is divorce and if fault lies with the husband.[9] In Xinjiang also, bride-price (*lote*) was claimed and received.[10] It needs mention that the payment of the bride-price was common in the Gandhar and Madra regions of western Punjab and Afghanistan during the *Mahabharata* days. Bhishma paid the bride-price for the Madri to the king of Madra for her marriage to Pandu.[11] Rishi Richik gave 1,000 special kind of horses to king Gadhi as the bride-price of Satyavati.[12]

Puri, on the other hand, provides the mixed picture so far as the status of women in the region was concerned. In one hand, he writes that "As a part of the family, she has no doubt her position, but being treated as the property of her husband she could be given in exchange, or be saleable commodity and her value was determined by her height and in cash or in kind (nos. 587, 437), etc. As part of the sale transaction or gift (no. 380), or in exchange (no. 551), as also for payment of debt (no. 114), she could be transferred to the other party without hindrance." On the other hand, he refers to the women's rights to amass money, non-payment of bride-price if the girl elopes with her suitor (no. 621), a monk's daughter, defying her father's wish, eloping with a potter's son (no. 621), dissolution of marriage (no. 34, 621) if not covered by the monetary payment to the girl's father, ladies of the upper strata of the society acquiring education and being capable of free communication with friends and relatives (no. 316). Moreover, tradition allowed the payment of bride-price (*lote*) and exchange marriage (*vinimaya*; no. 279, 481).[13] Burrow discusses a term *vivega*[14] — meaning probably separation (no. 34). All these present a mixed picture of the status of the women in the region, and the lack of cohesive analysis, rather than listing of the data.

Slavery

Slavery was prevalent in the region. The slaves – *dāsa* (no. 345, 491), *dāsī* (6210, *dajha* (569), *dhaja* (227), *dhajhī* (39, 45) were treated as the members of the family of the master (*bhatare*, no. 147; *bhatāraga*; Sanskrit – *bhaṭṭāraka*). A servant (*presi*; no. 204) formed different category. Yet *vathayaga* (*vadhaya*; no. 118; Khotanese – *vaksaya*; Tokharian - *upasthayak*), required to look after the grazing cattle, formed another category of domestic employee, who used to receive salary and perquisites — *parikraya bhojana* (*pacevara*; food) and clothes (*coḍaga*). In a record (no. 25), three *milim* rice and in another (no. 470) ten *khi* rice was mentioned as the remuneration for such an employee. A *prithabhārika* (Sanskrit – *priṣṭhabhārika*; no. 396) used to carry load on his back. Slaves and servants used to look after the farms, cattle and the domestic works of the master. Whereas the slave was bonded for the specified period of say ten years (no. 550) or twelve years (no 364), same was not the case with the servants. The breach of agreement by the slave was punishable (no. 764).[15]

Slaves formed marketable and presentable commodities (nos. 491, 324). Some inscriptions record the sale of girls and men (*pruṣdhaya*), transfer of ownership, as well as the right to sale, pledge, exchange and present the slaves (nos. 589, 590, 591). Slaves were punished for the crimes of theft (nos. 518, 345, 561); exemplary punishments even led to death (no. 144). Even the master was liable for the lapse of his slave (no. 345, 561). The slave had certain rights too. He could purchase his freedom by paying back the *lote* and *mukeśi* to his master (no. 585); could earn some money, cattle and clothes, and his master was not allowed to appropriate the same (nos. 24, 327); he was allowed to adopt someone with the consent of the master. The monks also kept slaves to look after their farms and property interests (no. 152).[16]

Professions, Agriculture and Material Culture

Kharosthi documents mention about the various professions of the region, such as, *kammakarejamna* (manual unskilled worker; Sanskrit —*karmakār*, Pāṇini: 3,2,22; Bhojpuri—*kamkar*), sculptor (*silpig*; Sanskrit—*śilpi*), carpenter (*dacchamna* or *tacchamna*; Sanskrit—*takṣan*), bow-maker (*dhaṃnukar*, Sanskrit—*dhanuṣkar*), arrow-maker (*kaḍa-kara*; Sanskrit—*kāṇḍākara*), potter (*kulala*; Sanskrit - *kulāla*), goldsmith (*suvarnakara*; Sanskrit—*suvarṇakāra*), porter (*prithabharige*; Sanskrit—*pṛṣṭha-bhāraka*). Numerous Kharosthi documents relate to land deeds, court decisions about the sale, transfer and ownership of the land, marking of boundaries, ploughing, sowing, quality of the land (*bhuma, buma. bhumi*; Sanskrit - *bhūmi*), arable land (*bhuma-chetra* or *bhuma-chitra*; Sanskrit – *Bhūmī-kṣetra*), farm land (*gotha bhuma*), sandy land (*sigata bhuma*; Sanskrit – *sikatā bhūmī*), waste land (*vyartha-bhuma*; Sanskrit – *vyartha bhūmī*), season of sowing seed (*biji, bhija, bhisa*, etc.; Sanskrit - *bīja*), need of irrigation, etc. There was a belief among the Niya people, as mentioned in Kharosthi document no. 565, that ploughing, sowing and tilling of vine yards during the Pig Nakssatra were certainly to be fruitful (*sugara nichhatravavana masu ṣaḍa uchavina sidhi-vardhi bhaviṣyati*). As per document no. 450, spring season (*vasaṁta*) was considered suitable for cultivation (*vasaṃtaṃmi karamnae*). Irrigation channels were not only in existent in eastern, but also in western Turkistan, and water used to be diverted from one channel to the other for irrigation (*Kṛṣivatrami udaga nasti anodaka huta, ahuno teṣa rajaṃni nivartavidavya*; no 125).[17]

Domestic animals were part of the economy of the region. They served the purpose of food, transport, leather, wool, gift and exchange. The most of the terms used for them, as well as for wild beasts, were Prakrit or Sanskrit. *Stora, paśu* and *jaṃdu* (Sanskrit—*jantu*) meant animal. The words for them are: camel (*uṭa*; Sanskrit *uṣṭra*), horse (*aspa*; Sanskrit—*aśva*), mare (*vaḍavi*; Sanskrit—*vāḍavā*), cow (*go*), deer (*mṛga*), ass (*khara*), dog (*sūna*; Sanskrit—*śvāna*), fox (*lomaṭi*; Sanskrit—*lomaṭaka*; Hindi - *lomaḍi*), lion (*kesari*; no. 103; *siṃgha*, Sanskrit—*sinha*, no. 511), tiger (*vyāgra*, Sanskrit – *vyāghra*, no. 565). Camel had about two dozen other epithets in Niya Prakrit. There were different terms for pregnant cow (*go garbhina*, no. 186), large cow (*go mahatṃa*, no. 122), calve of cow (*gavi savatse*, no. 7), royal cows (*ravaka gaviyan*, no. 159), cow enclosure (*go śaḍaṃni*), etc.[18]

Food Items

The terms for many food items used to be Indian. Cooked rice (*bhata*; Sanskrit—*bhakta*), rice (*taṃdula*; Sanskrit—*taṇḍula*), wheat (*gohomi*; Sanskrit—*godhum*; Hindi - *gehun*), barley (*yavi*; Sanskrit—*yava*, Hindi—*jau, jai*), sugar (*sakar*, Sanskrit—*sarkarā*; Hindi—*sakkar*), salt (*sidha—lavaṇa*; Sanskrit—*lavaṇa*), pepper (*marica*), ginger (*aridaga*; Hindi—*adarak*), ghee (*ghṛda*; Sanskrit—*ghṛta*; Hindi—*ghee*); small cardamons (*susmala, pipali*); fruits (*phalophala*; *phalaj phala, Sanskrit*); pomegranate (*daḍima*; Sanskrit—*daḍima*); *Ghṛtakumbha* used for storage jar for ghee is also used in Sanskrit and Hindi in India). The word for food in Niya Prakrit is *bhoyaṃna* (Sanskrit—*bhojana*; Hindi—*bhojan*).[19] The staple food consisting of wheat, rice and corn, generally called *pacewara,* was used as flour (*ata-ata* and *saktū*; no. 359) and rice (*dhānya*). Several inscriptions record the common use of spirituous liquor (nos. 175, 244, 317, 329, 343); old wine was used by the king; common people used restricted limit of only three *khi* of ordinary wine. There is no mention of wine-shops or bar; the wine supplied to the ruler had to be sealed. Production of wine was, however, subjected to taxation. An inscription (no. 478) mentions that the provisions were made for the soldiers in the capital in the form of corn and sheep. An inscription (nos. 478, 641) further records that food was meant to sustain the body and one's existence (*nisaganam*).[20]

Dress and Ornaments

The Kharosthi documents and the statues and paintings provide adequate information about the dress and ornaments of the people of the region. The words for wool, hemp and roll of silk in Niya Prakrit are *urṇa, saṃna* and *paṭa* respectively. *Cama* or *carma* (Sanskrit—*carma*) denoted leather. The book written on leather was called *carma-pothi* (Sanskrit—*carm-pustaka*). Here, it needs mention that *pothi* is widely used in India for the book. *Kojaya* (Pali—*kojava*), *veda* (as in *Cina-veda*) and *cotaga* were the terms for rug, turban and upper garment respectivcly; the term for bodice (Sanskrit—*kanchulika*) was *kamculi* or *kamjuliya. Goni* was used for sack, and *raju* or *rasamna* for rope.[21]

Male and female alike used the coat or upper covering, called cotaga or codaga. (nos. 19, 506). The ladies used a trouser and a petticoat type of covering (*pamzavanta*) made of *prigha,* a particular kind of silk (no. 318). *Candri-kammata* (nos. 272, 714), according to Bailey,[22] was a kind of trouser made from a sheet of cloth. *Cina-cimar* (no. 149; Sanskrit—*Cina-civara*) is the Chinese over-coat, whereas *civara* is the Buddhist monk's upper covering. The Indian blanket (*kambala*) was *loyi* (Hindi—*loyi*), also known as *kojava* (nos. 583, 593, 599).[23] In an inscription (no. 149), there is mention of a silver ornament, and in another one (no. 566), there is mention of seven-stringed pearl/ornament (*muṭilaṭā*) and one ear pendant (*sudī*).[24] *Pagri* was white turban.

Religion and Polity

Xinjiang, in particular and Central Asia in general, was a part of India Central Asia Iran religio-cultural-linguistic continuum. Buddhism predominated. Of course, Hinduism preceded Buddhism in the region. This aspect is discussed elsewhere in the book. The Buddhists, as described in the documents, used to lead a very rich life, possessed landed property and slaves. These monks, residing in the monasteries (*viharas, sangaramas*) were, however, not allowed to attend the *posatha* ceremony in the dress of a householder (*grihasatacodin*; no. 489). Some terms used in the documents are: *Śramana, samana, thera, sthaira* (for *sthavira*), *bhighu, bhuchu, bhichu* (for *bhikshu*), *Bhichu-samga* (for *Bhikṣu-saṅgha*) and *bramaṃna* (for a *Brāhmaṇa*).[25]

Politics

The king was called *maharaya* (Sanskrit – *mahārāja*; the great king). While addressing him, in the state injunctions and letters, or even in the coins, a series of charming titles and epithets were used for him, i.e. *maharayasa, rayatirayasa, mahaṃtasa, javaṃtasa, dhramaiasa sachadhamastidasa prachachhadevada nauva maharaya devaputras* (no. 655). The king was righteous, 'stable in true *dharma*', deity-incarnate, etc. He believed in piety and judgment according to *dharma* (*dhammen nico kartavo*; no. 1). It needs mention that King was considered to be the incarnation of Lord Viṣṇu, according to Hindu mythology. Some terms used in the Kharosthi documents, needing mention here, are: *Devi* for the queen, *maharaya-putra* for the prince, *raji jaṃna* for state officials, *seniya jaṃna* for the army people, and *duta* or *dutiya* (Sanskrit—*dūta*) for the ambassador. Official letters were sent through special messengers (*chara puruṣa*; no. 310). The state injunctions and letters of command (*anathi/ anadi/anada lekha*; in Indian literature—*Ājñaptilekha/Ājñapatra*) were duly sealed, as available in wedge-shaped tablets, designed as *anati-kilmuṃdra* (Sanskrit—*kīla mudrā*). Secret communications were made through *vinatilekhas* (*pravṛttika* letters in Indian literature) during the periods of upheavals. The official correspondence formally began with the common phrase *mahanuava maharaya lihati.*[26] But all the letters did not follow it, as Stein writes: "official custom knew also a style far less ornate is amply shown by businesslike and peremptory tone adopted in some of the wedge-shaped tablets, ordering submission of affidavits accordi..g to a special list, production of certain witness, arrests of certain individuals, etc."[27]

The system of taxation was highly organized. The taxes could be paid in cash and kind—in corn, other farm products, ghee, wine, camels, textiles, garments, blankets, carpets, felt, etc. There were state officials for maintaining the records as well as for the collection of the taxes. Indian currency, such as *masaka* and *masa* (nos. 661, 149, 500), and *suvarṇa* and *kanaka* for gold, find mention along with Persian and Greek currencies.[28]

Extended Linguistic Links

It needs mention that the linguistic links between India and Xinjiang was far more extensive than covered in this chapter. The Kharosthi documents reveal similarities at the syntactical, phonetic and lexical level, which need further in-depth study. Like in India, textiles was measured by 'hand' (*hasta*, Hindi — *hāth*= 18 inches). Human height was measured by *diṭhis* or *tiṭhis* (span; Sanskrit -*diṣṭi*) and the land by the measurement of seed required. Terms, such as, *adha* (half; Sanskrit — *ardha*; Hindi—*ādhā*), *pada* (a quarter; Sanskrit—*pāda*) and *matra* (quantity; Sanskrit—*mātrā*) were also in use. The words used for different colours—*pita* (yellow; Sanskrit — *pīta*), *nila* (blue; Sanskrit—*nīla*), *paṃḍura* (white or yellow; Sanskrit— *pāṇḍura*), *raṭaga* (red; Sanskrit—*rakta/rakta varṇa*), *speta* (white; Hindi—*saphed*), *nila-raṭaga* (red-blue; Sanskrit—*nīla-rakta*) also need to be mentioned here.[29]

Local Impact on the Script and the Language

Although the Gandhari Prakrit has close agreement with the post-Asokan Kharosthi inscriptions of north-western India, it was also subjected to local and Iranian language influences. This Prakrit differs from other Prakrits according to the degree of modifications in its inflectional system. Gandhari Prakrit of the region has also the loan words from Iranian, Sogdian, Greek, Tibetan, Kuchean,

Uighur and other languages. The Krorainic phonetic structure affected the pronunciation of its words leading to several innovations in its script, such as, sign for expressing long vowels absent in the Prakrit of north-west India. The forms of several letters (*ka, ga, ca,* etc.) were modified and certain compound letters were devised to enable recording of local pronunciation.[30]

Scholarly Pursuits

It is a established fact that Gandhari Prakrit had a fairly extensive literature. Fragments of the Prakrit recension of the Dhammapada written in Kharosthi in the second century A.D., discovered in 1892 and 1897 in Khotan, make it the oldest surviving manuscript in any Indian language other than Sanskrit and Pali. Some inscriptions (nos. 501, 510) contain literary pieces. One inscription (no. 514) includes grammar, music, astronomy, the technique of writing poetry, etc. among the subjects of study.[31]

Kharosthi documents mention about various branches of Indian scholarly knowledge. A person anxious to be proficient in grammar (*śabda*), music (*gandharva;* different spelling—*gamdarva*—in no. 565), astronomy (*jotiṣ*), poetry (*kāvya-karaṃna*), dancing (*tālave*), painting (*citrāgāram aḇhirajate*), knowledge about happenings on earth and in air (*bhumi-vata caride*), etc. is depicted in no. 514; there is reference of 12 *nakṣatras* in no. 565. No. 523 describes the unstable nature of the riches thus: "just as a man travelling on journey rests here and there whenever overcome by fatigue, so a man's riches having rested from time to time come back again (*yathā manuṣyaḥ pathi vartamānaḥ kvacit kvacid viśramate śramārttaḥ, tathā manuṣyasya dhanāni kāle-kāle saṃmaśvāsya punar vrajanti*). It further refers to a prayer for victory and prosperity: *śata subhichu bhavatu samakula Imiraṃ vivṛdhi abhivarṣatu makhi udeṃtu śasya cha jayāya pārthiva ciraṃ sadhamaṣugata tiṣṭhatu.*[32]

Prakrit Languages and Kharosthi Script in Western Turkistan and Afghanistan : Their Historical Time-depth

The use of Prakrit language and Kharosthi script have been reported from many other places of Western Turkistan and Afghanistan, such as, inscriptions at Fayaz Tepe and Kara Tepe near Termez in

Tajikistan, inscriptions on gold slabs at Dalverzin Tepe in Uzbekistan, and the inscriptions discovered at Wardak and Kunduz in Afghanistan. The language and the script was used for secular dealings also, as the records of Dasht-e-Nawur in Afghanistan and gold slab inscriptions of Dalverzin Tepe exhibit.[33] The earliest usc of the Prakrit language in Kharosthi script goes back to first century B.C.[34] The use of a different variety of Prakrit, called variously as Sulika, Culika, Culika-Paisaci or Sogdian Prakrit[35] has currently in Samarkaṇd region.

References

1. *BSOAS,* London IX, pp. 111-25.
2. Agrawal, R.C., Some Aspects of Indian Culture in the Kharosthi Documents from Chinese Turkestan, in Lokesh Chandra *et al.*, (Ed.), *India's Contribution to World Thought and Culture,* p. 275.
3. Puri, B.N.; *Buddhism in Central Asia,* p. 232.
4. Agrawal, *op. cit,* p. 277.
5. Puri, B.N.; *op. cit.*, p. 232.
6. Agrawal, *op. cit.*, p. 277.
7. Puri, B.N.; *op. cit.*, p. 233.
8. Agrawal, *op. cit.*, p. 277.
9. Kumar, B.B.; *India: Caste, Culture and Traditions,* p. 91; also see chapter and annexure on the marriage in *The Tribal Societies* by the same author.
10. Puri, *op. cit.*, p. 234.
11. *Mahābhārata, Ādi Parva,* 112.9-16.
12. *Ibid., Anushāsan Parva,* 4.18.
13. Puri, *op. cit.*, pp. 214-15.
14. Burrow, *Language of the Kharosthi Documents from Chinese Turkistan,* Cambridge, 1937, p. 116.
15. Puri, *op. cit,* pp. 235-36.
16. *Ibid,* p. 236
17. Agrawal, *op. cit.*, pp. 178-79.
18. *Ibid.*, p. 278.
19. *Ibid.*, p. 280.
20. Puri, *op. cit.*, pp. 236-37.
21. Agrawal, *op. cit.*, p. 280.
22. *BSOAS,* Vol. XI, p. 793.
23. Puri, *op. cit.* pp. 237-38.
24. *Ibid.*, p. 240.
25. Agrawal, *op. cit.*, p. 280.

26. Agrawal, pp. 275-76.
27. Stein, A., *Ancient Khotan*, p. 36.
28. Agrawal, *op. cit.*, pp. 279-80.
29. *Ibid.*, p. 280.
30. *The Cultural Heritage of India*, Calcutta (1991), pp.704-05.
31. *Ibid.*, p. 705.
32. Agrawal, *op. cit.*, p. 278.
33. *The Cultural Heritage of India*, pp.706-07.
34. *Ibid.*, p. 706.
35. Bagchi, Prabodh Chandra; *India and Central Asia*, Calcutta (1955), pp. 141-51.

11

India and Central Asia : The Linguistic Links

Indo-Central Asian relations have been multi-dimensional and continuous starting from pre-historic time to the modern day. Our links cover linguistic area also. Central Asian and Indian languages have influenced each other; we speak many sister languages, as far example Tajik, Hindi and Urdu. Some scholars have discovered Indian language in use in Central Asia, such as Parya.

The Urdu language owes its origin to the Indo-Central Asian contact during the medieval period. 'Urdu' itself is a Persianized Turkish word, which originally meant 'the camp of a Turkish army'. In India, it means 'court' or 'camp'. The language, in its initial stages, was known as 'Hindi' or language of Hind or India'. It was also known as 'Hindwi' or 'Hindostani'. This language travelled to different places of India with Sufis or Muslim mystics, freely accepted various regional or local influences, and was also known as Gujari, Dakhni or Dehlavi.[1] Hindi language was also influenced by Turkic language. The number of Turkic words in Hindi, according to Dr. Bhola Nath Tiwari, a noted scholar, is not less than 125. Some of the Turkic words use in Hindi language are: Urdu, Bahadur, Uzbak, Turk, Chaku (knife), Kainchi (scissors), Qabu (in control), Chammach (spoon), Top (cannon), Topachi (gunner), Barud (gun-powder), Biwi (wife), Chechak (small-pox), Lash (dead body), Sarai (inn) and Bewarchi (cook). Suffix 'chi' of Turkic language is very much in use in Hindi.[2]

Hindi has large number of Turkic, Persian and Arabic words. Other Indian languages also have the words from these languages. Persian was the official language of India during the Mughal rule. Russian scholars have discovered some Indic languages in Central Asia. Pariah of Hissar Valley speak an Indic language of the same name in their homes. They communicate in Uzbek and Tajik languages with their neighbours.[3]

Central Asia is a polyglot society. Different languages were spoken in Tarim and Oxus valleys. Linguistic scene, however, did not remain the same at all the time in that region. The language scenario changed with the change in the ethnic composition with passage of time. Two languages were spoken in the early centuries of the Christian era in Xinjiang. The northern language was named Kuchean. It was also called Tokharian or the language of the Tokharas or Indo-Scythians. The language, with two great western and eastern groups, was supposed to be an Indo-European language. The language spoken in southern Tarim basin was called 'Saka' and 'Khotanese'. The three other languages, written in the script of Aramaic origin, were Iranian languages. Two of them have preserved Manichean texts. Sogdian, the language of the region around Samarkand contained Buddhist, Manichaean and Christian texts.[4]

Uighur, literary form of the various Turkish idioms spoken in north and south of Tien Shan, derived its name from the Uighur script, derived from the Syriac. It was widely used for Buddhist, Manichaean and Christian literature. Its use for Buddhist literature increased when Uighurs replaced Tibetan power in Tarim valley in about 860 A.D. and founded their own kingdom. Tibetan manuscripts have also been found in Khotan, Miran and Tun-huang regions. Prakrit recension of Dharmapada, and other documents, known as Kharoshthi documents, have been excavated from Xinjiang. The language (Gandhari Prakrit) and the script (Kharoshthi) of the same are Indian. Wide use of Sanskrit in Central Asia, especially by the Sarvastivadin Buddhists, is a well known fact. Khotanese, Agnean, Kuchean, Sogdian, Uighur, Turkish, Mongol, Manchu and Chinese manuscripts or tracts or the fragments have been recovered from Central Asia.[5]

Presently, Turkic languages are spoken in Uzbekistan, Kazakhstan and Kirghij Republic and Turkmenistan. Tajik spoken in Tajikistan is an Iranian language. Uighur is a Turkic language. Some religious minorities speak their own languages.

Apart from the scripts mentioned above, Brahmi was widely used in Central Asia. Its introduction in Central Asia and association with Buddhism is supposed to be of earlier date than that of

Kharoshthi. Three varieties of this script are traced in Sanskrit texts found there. The script was also used for writing Agnean (language of Agnidesha), Kuchean and Saka-Khotanese.[6]

The discoveries of an inscription of the first century B.C. in Tazikistan and an inscription on gold slab found at Dalverzin in Uzbekistan and some other inscriptions at Wardak and Kunduz in Afghanistan take us back before the Christian era, so far the use of Prakrit is concerned. As mentioned earlier, Kharoshthi documents were discovered from various archaeological sites in the Tarim basin, in Khotan, Niya, Endere, Miran, Lou-lan and Kurak Darya. Over two hundred documents written in black ink in Kharoshthi script on different materials — wood, leather, silk and paper — were discovered. Sir Aurel Stein wrote: "At the Niya site, I found hundred wooden documents comprising correspondence, mainly official, contracts, accounts, miscellaneous memoranda and the like, all written in Sanskrit language and the Kharoshthi script which during the first centuries before and after Christ were used on the Indian north-west frontier and in the adjacent portions of Afghanistan.[7] The inscriptions received at Miran were fresh even after the lapse of two thousand years. A large number of coins struck in Khotan or nearby places were also in the same script. The coins dated first century B.C. to first century A.D."[8]

Sanskrit was methodically taught in Central Asia. It was called 'Arshi' (Arya) in Tokharian. Many Sanskrit manuscripts, like that of Ashvaghosha's *Buddha Charit* and *Saundaranand Kavys* (discovered from Shorchuq), were found out in Central Asia during various excavations. Almost all the important Buddhist texts were translated in all the major Central Asian languages. The scholars not only studied the texts and translated them, but also wrote commentary on the texts. Grammar, astronomy and all other subjects were methodically taught and studied. Bower manuscripts discovered at Kucha are medical texts.

The languages of India and Central Asia had profound impact on each other. Genesis and development of Urdu and Turkic lexemes in Hindi are the results of Indian and Central Asian contact. Sanskrit has also the profound impact on the languages of Central Asia. The language of the region also had impact on Sanskrit. The Shaka and Slav languages, which were spoken in Central Asia, were intimately linked with Sanskrit. The relation of Turkic languages with the Aryan languages is very ancient.[9] Caldwell has given voluminous data and massive analysis of the links of the Turk-Mongol languages with South Indian language in general, in his *A Comparative Grammar of the Dravidian of South Indian Family of Language.* The work, however, had many shortcomings. Caldwell links Dravidian languages with the Sythian languages of Central Asia. But, the Scythian is a very loose grouping and, therefore, his study lacks sharp focus.

Some valuable information about Indo-Central Asian linguistic links is also available in the *History of Central Asia* (written in Hindi by Rahul Sankrityayan. The vocabulary of Russian language given by him shows massive lexical similarity with Sanskrit. Here, it needs mention that the difference between the languages of *Rigveda* and *Avesta,* and that between Sanskrit and old Persian is mostly phonetic, and not grammatical. The Iranian languages of Central Asia and Iran are intimately related to the Indo-Aryan languages.

Dr. Ram Vilash Sharma, a well-known Indian scholar has brought many lexical, phonetic, morphological and syntactical similarities of Turkic and Mongol language with Indian languages in his Hindi publication, *Bharat ke Prachin Bhasha Parivar Aur Hindi.* Dr. Sharma compares the languages of Turk-Mongol and Fino-Ugrian families with the languages of India. He compares phonetic, lexical, morphological traits of Turkic, Mongol (Khalkh, Buriat) and Fin languages with those of the Indian languages.

Turkic, like many Indo-Aryan and Dravidian languages, shows the tendency of palatization. But unlike Dravidian and Indo-Aryan languages, it does not use cerebrals. Turkic adds semi-vowel 'y' before some vowels attached to 'k' and 'g'. Arabian words '*katib*' (secretary), '*malum*' (known) and '*majkur*' (said earlier) become *kyatip, malum* and *majkyur* respectively. This trait is found in Kashmiri also. Here 'a' in '*majkur*' is shortened. The 'b' of '*katib* becomes 'p'. Arabic '*kitab*' and Sanskrit '*rang*' become '*kitap*' and '*rank*' in Turkic language. Thus 'b' and 'k' are devoiced in that language. When pronominal suffix 'i' (his or her) is added, then 'p' is again voiced and the word becomes '*kitabi*'. This trait is visible in Sanskrit also, as we find in such words as 'Jagadish', 'sharadagam', etc. Like Dravidian languages, no word of Turkic has initial 'r' and 'l'. This tendency has become somewhat lax in Dravidian languages. Tamil '*irandu*' (two) is sometimes spoken as '*randu*'. 'Reddy' is the name of a caste in Andhra Pradesh. Turkic and Dravid languages usually do not use two consonants together in the beginning of a word.

'Slav' is pronounced 'Islav' (as 'school' is pronounced 'iskul' in eastern India) in Turkic. English word 'club' is pronounced 'kulup' or 'klup'. Like Prakrit, some mid-consonants become vowels or semi-vowels. Persian 'agar' (if) and 'digar' become 'ayar' and 'diyar'. Fricative 'f' in borrowed Persian words becomes 'p' in Turkic languages. Fricative 'kh' of Arabic and Persian words usually becomes 'h'. Arabic 'fun' (art), khala (mother's sister), 'khabar' (news) and Persian 'hafta' (week) become 'pan, 'hala', 'habar' and 'hapta' respectively. Like Dravidian languages, the use of aspirates is not the trait of the Turkic languages. Most of the Indian languages use dental and palatal sibilants — s and sh (ś). Cerebral sibilant 'sh' (ṣ) is used mostly in Sanskrit words. The Aryan and Dravidian languages, and to some extent Turkic, has the tendency to convert dental and palatal sibilant into palatal 'ch' and 'chh'. In Sanskrit, the roots 'gash' gaś, गाश्(gam, to go) and 'prash' praś, प्रश् (to ask; prashna, question) become 'gachchh' and 'prachchh' respectively. Sanskrit 'bhash' bhāṣ, भाष्becomes 'peshu' पेशु in Tamil; the Sanskrit root 'ish' इष् (ish, iṣ, to drink) is transformed into 'ich' (drink) into Turkic.

Dr. Ram Vilash Sharma has pointed towards many similarities and parallels at lexical level. Turkic lexemes for Sanskrit 'kar' (to do), 'kal' (time), 'kup'(well), 'kati' (how many), 'kim' (who) are 'kil' (old Turkic), 'kara', 'kuyu', 'kach' and 'kim'. Turkic 'kara' (black), Tamil 'karu' and Sanskrit 'kar' (of 'andhakar) are related. Hindi uses relative suffix 'ka, ki, ke'; in Turkic, it is 'ki'. 'Janma' (birth) of Sanskrit is derived from the root 'jan'. In Turkic, 'dagum' (birth) and 'ichim' are derived from 'dagh' (to be born) and 'ich' (to drink). Turkic, Tamil and Russian languages use relative suffix '–in' as in 'Ahamadin' (of Ahmad; Turkic), Maganin (of the son) and Stalin (of steel). Negative suffix –ma in Sanskrit and –ma in Turkic is identical.

The Indian languages, except Khasi and Kashmiri, follow 'Subject-object-verb' syntactical pattern. Turkic language also follows the same. However, like in Sanskrit in "gachchhami' (I go; gachchh, to go); in Turkic 'galiriṃ' (I come); the pronominal suffix follows the verb. Neither Sanskrit 'ami' or 'mi', nor Turkic 'im' are freely used as first person singular pronoun, I, as is done in Bengali and Marathi. The word for 'I' in the Sanskrit and Turk languages is 'aham' and 'ban' respectively. Turkic language uses pronominal suffix after the noun as in 'babam' (my father; baba=father, -m=my).

It needs mention that 'Baba' is also used for father in many Indian Languages. The pattern of adding pronominal suffix as well as the suffix for 'I' in this case is of Indian origin. Arabic and Persian also follow the same. Both Hindi and Turkic add the verb denoting 'to do' to the noun to make verb ('karana' in Hindi, 'kam karna', to do the work; 'kilmak' in Turkic, 'namaj kilmak', to do or perform namaj).

In many cases, new meaning comes when two words are added and density of meaning is achieved by re-duplication of words. The pattern of the formation of higher numerals in Turkic, Dravidian and many Munda and Indo-Mongoloid languages is the same.[10]

New discoveries in Central Asia and India during colonial days have brought out huge material about the culture and languages of the two regions. However, the colonial studies have also many drawbacks. In many cases, the cultural and linguistic continuum, both in terms of time and geographical spread was ignored; differences, rather than the similarities were emphasized.

Many geographical names and names of the communities of Central Asia found in our Classical literature and epics have not yet changed or have changed slightly. Kubha, Gomati Oxus and Kandahar are as yet known as Kabul, Gomal, Oxus and Gandhar.

The last syllable of the Central Asian nations is 'stān'. It is related to the Sanskrit 'sthān' and Persian 'stān', denoting land or place. Kāśyapa was a seer and progenitor of the living world according to the Indian mythology. Phrigia is called Phrugia in Greek. Indian literature has Bhrigu, a seer. I am not sure whether 'Phoenic' of the word 'Phoenician' can be derived from Semitic roots. Sanskrit has the word 'Banik', the trader. I feel the deep study of the languages and cultures of Central Asia may help Indians in understanding themselves better. The reverse may be equally true.

Panini in his *Ashtadhyayi* has mentioned the word *kanthā*. The word in *Kashikā Sūtra* denotes 'town' or 'city'. The 'kand' or 'kent'of Tashkent, Samarkand, Yarkand, etc. is the same as the above-mentioned *kanthā*. Tashkent and Yarkand, I am told, were also known as 'Dākshikānthā' and 'Yahvarkanthā' respectively. The Sanskrit word for 'Turk' is *Turuṣka.* The first syllable of the name is found in the name of 'Turvasu' in classical Indian literature. The second syllable 'ṣka' is a superlative ṣuffix found in the name of Kaniṣka; the meaning of 'Kaniṣka' is the youngest son.[11]

Tashkent, the capital city of Uzbekistan, and Samarkand, the ancient capital of Sogdiana and that of Timur and Babar, are ancient cities. The old name of Tashkent is Chach. Pulleyblank wanted to connect it with Yenisseian word for 'stone': Ket. *Tyes,* Kot. *shish,* Pumpokolsk *cys.* He sees it as a relic of the Hun occupation of the Sogdiana in the fifth and sixth centuries. However, as the word finds place in the inscriptions of Shapur I (240-272 A.D.) and therefore, it had earlier currency. In the old Chinese records, Tashkent is transcribed with the hieroglyph '*shih'* that is stone. The name is linked with Turkic *tash,* 'stone' and may be considered a translation of the older names of the city. It is pointed out that the older names of the city before '*Chach*' also had the meaning 'stone'. The inhabitants of the area, according to Chinese sources, were *Ch'iang chu* or *K'ang chu,* very likely of Tukharian origin. *K'ang* may mean some kind of stone in Tokharian. In Hindi, '*kankar* is pebble. According to *Sutrālaṁkāra,* a painter of Pushkalawati visited the country *Ashmaka* (meaning stone or stony) and out of his piety decorated a Buddhist monastery. The place is identified with Tashkent. There was a tradition that *Sutralamkar* was written by Ashvaghosha. Others attribute its authorship to Kumarlat, the founder of *Sautrantika* school of Buddhism. Ashmak, was the name of a north-western country, according to the *Brihatsaṁhitā* of Varahamihira. Kumarajiva knew the great cities of the North like Alasanda and Tashkent.[12] It needs mention that the word *Tashkent* first appears in *Ta'rikh al-Hind* of al-Beruni.[13]

References

1. Mansura Haider, *India and Central Asia: Linkages and Interactions*; in Nirmala Joshi's Central Asia, p. 261.
2. *The Cultural Heritage of India,* Vol. V, pp. 642-43.
3. B.N. Puri, *Buddhism in Central Asia,* pp. 141-43.
4. *Ibid.*, p. 325.
5. *Ibid.*, p. 242-43.
6. I.M. Oranskii, 'An Essay on the Ethnography of a group of Indic Language Speaking Pariah (in the Hissar Valley), in *India and Central Asia'* by Surendra Gopal, pp. 139-42.
7. Bhola Nath Tiwari, *Hindi Bhasha,* pp. 179-81.
8. *Ibid.*, pp. 182-84.
9. *Ibid.*, p. 186-87.
10. Aurel Stein, *Ancient Central Asian Tracts,* Maṣṭillan & Co., London, 1955, p. 28.
11. Communicated by Professor Lokesh Chandra during personal communication.
12. Penti Aalto, Helsinki, *The Name of Tashkent.*
13. *Ibid.*

12

Central Asian Buddhist Savants

Two earliest lay disciples of Buddha from Tokharestan, according to Hiuan-tsang, were Trapusa and Bhallika. They were merchants, natives of the kingdom of Balhika. While in India for trade, they happened to be at Bodhgaya at the time the Buddha had just attained his enlightenment. Asoka speaks of his efforts to introduce Buddhism among three neighbouring people of Gandhara, Kamboja and Yona. The roles of Demetrius, Menander and Asoka's descendants in protecting Buddhism and that of Kaniṣka in the spread of faith are well-known. The city of Balkh, also known as 'Little Rajagṛha', as Hiuan-tsang said, had Navasaṅghārāma (also called Navavihāra), the greatest centre of learning in the north of the Hindukush. As Hiuan-tsang states, the Navasaṅghārāma of Balhika was "the only Buddhist establishment in the north of the Hindukush, in which there was a constant succession of Masters who were commentators of the canon". Built by a former king of Balkh, it was located outside the city towards its south-west. Its administration was in the hands of Barmakid family; they governed an estate of 8 farsakh in length and 4 in width. Its high priests were called Paramaka (Barmaka); they were converted to Islam and went to Baghdad, played great role in the field of scholarship even after their conversion. As ministers of Harun-al-Rashid, they exercised great influence on the cultural life of the capital, Baghdad; they were responsible for sending ambassadors to India in search of Sanskrit books of astronomy, mathematics and medicine; got them translated into Arabic, which gave an impetus to the scientific investigation in the Arab world. The Buddhism flourished in Tokharestan, at least from second century up to the beginning of the eighth century, till slightly after the destruction of that great centre of learning, called Nawbahar (Navavihara) by the Arabs in the end of seventh century.[1]

Tokharestan, even when Buddhism was passing through the

stage of decline when Hiuan-tsang passed through the region, has numerous monasteries, stupas and convents. There was a very famous old convent in the neighbourhood of Navavihara, frequented by the people from distant lands. Navavihara's main hall contained a beautiful image of Buddha. There were 27 principalities in spite of Turk rule; there were some Buddhist monasteries with a few monks in every state. Balkh, as Hiuan-tsang wrote, had about 100 monasteries with more than 3,000 monks. Termez had 10 monasteries with about 1,000 monks; Kunduz had about 10 monasteries with a few hundred monks; in Gaz, there were about 10 monasteries with only about 100 monks. The situation was better in Tarim basin. In some places, there were both Mahayanists and Hinayanists, i.e. in Kunduz; in Gaz, there were only the followers of Hinayana school of the Sarvastivada school.[2] In Tarim basin, Sanskrit Hinayana literature have been found in Kucha and Agnidesha (Agnideśa), and Mahayana literature in Khotan, Kashgar and Kucha.

Central Asia has been an intellectually fertile soil. As discussed above, Barmaks of Central Asia intellectually fertilized and vitalized the Arabs. The Central Asian *Vaibhāṣik* scholars, and later on scholars like Al-Biruni, Al-Khwarezmi and Al-Shina, achieved great intellectual heights.

Among the Buddhist scholars of Central Asia, there were some scholars, who were born in India and elsewhere. But there were a large number of the native Central Asian scholars also. Ghoṣaka, one of the two famous Buddhist scholars of Tokharestan of the Kushan period, took an important part in the discussions on abstruse subjects by great Buddhist scholars, held under the supervision of Pārśva in the Buddhist council of Puruṣapura (Peshawar) convoked by Kanishka. The *Vibhaṣa,* a stupendous commentary of the *Abhidharmapiṭaka* of the Sarvāstivāda school was compiled in that council. Apart from the above-mentioned work, he also composed an original treatise on *Abhidharma,* known as *Abhidharmāmṛta,* which is one of the most clear expositions of the doctrine of *Abhidharma.* The Chinese translation of the book, made in the third century, is found up till now. The school following *Vibhasa,* called *Vaibhāṣika,* was divided later on in sub-schools, one of which was *Pascātya* (Western) Vaibhāṣika, connected with Balkh.[3]

Kumāralāta was a famous Buddhist savant of Central Asia, the manuscript of whose book *Kalpanā-maṇḍiṭikā* or *Kalpanā-maṇḍiṭikā-dṛṣṭāntapaṅkti* was recovered from Kucha and Turfan. H. Luders attributed authorship of Aśvaghoṣa's *Sutrālaṁkār* also to him, finding similarity of its Chinese version by Kumarajiva with Kumaralata's *Kalpanā-maṇḍiṭikā.* Yet, others suggest that the author of *Sutrālaṁkār* was Aśvaghoṣa, and Kumaralāta only expanded it by the addition of moral lessons and apologues in the form of examples according to the practice of the *Darṣṭantikā* School. It needs mention that Kumaralāta was a famous Buddhist scholar of the *Sautrāntika* School and founder of its *Dārstāntika* branch. According to Buddhist tradition, Kumaralāta was 'the sun shining in the North, while Aśvaghoṣa illuminated the East, Nāgārjuna the West and Āryadeva the South. As he was most famous as an author and founder of a school, he was forcibly taken to Kie-p'an-t'e. He was native of Takṣaśilā.[4]

Aśvaghoṣa and Mātriceṭa (*Mātṛcheṭa*) were famous scholars and poets of the region. Dharmaitra, a native of Termez on the Pakṣu of Tukhara country, was a Vaibhasika Acarya. Translation of his *Vinayasutrāntikā* is found in the Tanjur section of the Tibetan Buddhist canon. Āryacandra, who translated the *Maitreyasamiti* into the Tokharian language, was also a *Vaibhasika.* It needs mention that the Tokharian language manuscripts have been found from Kucha and Turfan regions and not from Tokharestan. This was perhaps due to their shifting to the former region due to Arab attack. A large number of scholars did the translation work from one language to another. The community of the translators of Sanskrit Buddhist texts into Chinese was marked by prefixing Che- for Yueh-che, Po- for Tukharas/Kucheans, Ngan- for Parthians and K'ang- for Sogdians. As for example, Che-Kien was a Yach-che Ngan-Se-Kao was a Parthian. Here it needs mention that the prefix An-(ngan-) has come from the old name of Parthia, An-she (Arsak) by the Chinese; K'ang from Kanka (Sanskrit—Kanka, Kanga; Chinese – K'ang-kiu). The term "Arjuna" formed part of the names of the kings of certain Tukhara dynasties of Tarim basin. Arjuna means 'white' in Sanskrit; the corresponding term in the Chinese is Po. The racial interpretation basing on the term 'po' meaning 'white' is, therefore, wide of reality. Tukharas, in reality, were the members of the Sanskrit speaking family, and cousins of Indians.

Buddhist scholars of different countries, including those of

Central Asia, played eminent role in the spread of Buddhism in various countries of the world. As discussed elsewhere in the book, the Central Asians' role in the spread of Indian culture, its music, musical instruments, mathematics, etc. have been equally noticeable. Buddhist savants of Central Asia and other cc ıntries worked to translate Buddhist texts into Chinese and other languages. Scholars translating Sanskrit Buddhist texts in different periods have been listed in Chinese Buddhist Tripitaka. According to the list of Nanjo[5], out of 72 such translators, working between 67 A.D. to 420 A.D., there were seven Yueh-chis (Tukharas), five Parthians, seven Kubhans (from Kabul or parts of Afghanistan), 15 Indians, 21 from the western countries and 17 Chinese; the 21 scholars from western countries included scholars from Khotan, Sogdhiana and other areas of Central Asia. It needs mention here that the Chinese counted India and Central Asia among the western countries. Among 43 scholars working from 420 A.D. to 550 A.D., 14 were Indians, 10 from Kubha (Kabul, Afghanistan) and Central Asian countries, four from Sri Lanka and South-East Asia, and four of unknown origin.[6]

A Parthian prince, Lokottama, called Ngan-Se-Kao by the Chinese historians, abdicated his throne in favour of his uncle; left his family, became a Buddhist monk at an early age, and arrived in the western frontier of China with a burden of books. Reaching Loyang in 144 A.D., he started preaching Buddhism. At Loyang, he settled down in the Monastery of Po-ma-sse (the White Horse Monastery) established by two pioneer Indian Buddhist monks, Dharmaratna and Kāśyapa Mātaṅga. They were the first Buddhist missionaries to China in 68 A.D., who met Chinese ambassador in Yue-che country. First of all, the Chinese ambassador Tsing Kiang received Buddhist texts as presents to the Chinese court in the year 2 B.C. from Tokharestan. Again, Ngan-Se-Kao was the first to come to China and establish a school of translators of Sanskrit Buddhist texts into Chinese. He was known as "Unrivalled". Many of the texts, translated by him, are extracts from the Buddhist *Agamas* illustrating the fundamental doctrines of Buddhism. He alone translated into Chinese more than a hundred Buddhist texts, out of which 55 are still available. Another Parthian, a merchant, named Ngan Hiuan, came to Loyang, received the imperial favour for rendering some valuable service to the public. He got the title of the "Chief Officer of the Cavalry". He, however, gave up all official distinctions soon, became Buddhist and then joined White Horse Monastery. Being a scholar, he collaborated in the translation work of the monastery. He also translated quite large number of texts into Chinese. The translators of the school of Ngan-Se-Kao included famous Indo-Scythian monk, Lokakṣema, some Sogdian monks and a Chinese priest, named Yen-Fo-T'iao. As a patient collaborator of Ngan Hiuan, he learnt Sanskrit, the sacred language of the Buddhist texts brought from Central Asia, was able to recite the whole of the *Pratimokṣa*; he was given the title of *Ācārya* and Sanskrit name Buddhadeva. After them, many other Parthian or Indo-Scythian monks also went to China and translated Buddhist texts in Chinese. Many Sogdian Buddhist monks also worked in China and helped Ngan-Se-Kao in his work of translation of Sanskrit texts into Chinese. Seng-hui (Sanghamati) was a Sogdian monk, who was the first to work in South China during third century A.D. His ancestors were first settled in India; his father, who was a merchant, stayed in Tonkin (Kiao-che), where he was born in the first quarter of the third century. He became a monk after the death of his father, went to Nanking; built a monastery and then founded a school there. He brought many Chinese to Buddhist faith; translated about a dozen books, out of which some are extant.[7]

Lokakṣema of Tukhara origin was a monk of rare learning. He went to Loyang in 147 A.D. and worked in China till 188; he translated some of the most important Buddhist texts in Chinese, some of which are still extant. Che Kien (190-220), a Tukharian and one of the young disciples of Lokakṣema, migrated out from North China due to political trouble and settled in Nanking. He worked there till mid-third century; translated over a hundred texts, out of which 49 are still available. Dharmarakṣa, a monk of Tukhara descent, who had travelled far and wide in Central Asia and learnt 36 different languages, settled in Tunhuang. Then he went to China in 284 A.D., worked till 313 A.D. and translated 200 Buddhist texts, out of which 90 are still available. She-lun, and Dharmanandi were also of Tukhara origin. She-lun went to China in 373 A.D. and translated four works. Dharmanandi, the last to go from Tukhara country to China in 384, translated many texts in Chinese out of which two, including *Ekkottarāgama*, is still found.[8]

Dharmasinha — Ta-mo-seng-kia, as Hiuan-tsang called him — was an excellent scholar of Vibhāṣa. Both met at Kunduz, which was a Centre of Buddhist learning when the latter visited that place. He was a widely travelled and highly educated person, went to India for education and also to the north of Hindukush. He was recognized as an authority on Buddhism, and a 'law-maker' by the Buddhists of different countries.

Kumarajiva, the son of a Kashmiri Brahman, Kumarayana, and Jiva, the princess of Kucha, was the most famous Buddhist scholar of Central Asia and China. He came to Kashmir (Kipin) for study when he was a young boy of seven and then returned to Kucha. While returning to Kucha, he stayed at Kashgar for a year and studied Abhidharmapiṭaka with the Kashmirian scholar Buddhayaśa, who was at that time there. He also studied the four *Vedas*, five sciences, Brahmanical sacred texts, astronomy, Saṭaśāstra, and the Madhyamaka Śastra etc. during his stay at Kashgar. It is at Kashgar that two princes of Cokkuka — Sūryabhadra and Sūryasena — went to receive initiation from Kumarajiva and to study Mahayana texts from him.[9]

Apart from Dharamratna and Kāśyapa Mātaṅga, the founders of 'White Horse Monastery', numerous Indians, such as Dharmagupta from South India, Punyatrāta and his disciple, Dharmayaśa from Kashmir, Guṇavarman and Buddhajiva from Kashmir, went to Central Asia and/or China, and either stayed there or returned. Vimalākṣa was a Śramaṇa of Kabul.

References

1. Bagchi, Prabodh Chandra, *India and Central Asia*, pp. 31-35.
2. *Ibid.*, pp. 34-35.
3. *Ibid.*, pp. 33-34.
4. *Cultural Heritage of India*, p. 713; note 26.
5. Puri, B.N., *Buddhism in Central Asia* (p. 86, note 1) informs about the catalogues based on Chinese sources, such as, *A Catalogue of the Chinese Buddhist Tripiluka*, Oxford (1882) Appendix II, pp. 379ff; Earnest J. Eitel (Reprint, Cosmos Publications, 1981; original edition 1888) refers to contributions of different scholars. B.A. Litvinsky recorded the calculation in his *Outline History of Buddhism in Central Asia* circulated at the Diushandbe session (1968) of the 'International Conference on the History, Archaeology and Culture of Central Asia in the Kushan Period, p. 13.
6. Puri, *op. cit.*, p. 87.
7. Bagchi, *op. cit.*, p. 37-40.
8. *Ibid.*, pp. 33-34.
9. Puri, *op. cit.*, pp. 81, note 108.

13

Anarchy in the Nomenclature: A Brief Note

A particular difficulty in the study of Central Asia has been the multiplicity of the names of the places, communities and even the individuals. Central Asia, as discussed elsewhere, has the record of the barbaric destruction of its intellectual wealth at least twice; once by the Alexander and next time by the Arab Governor Kutaib. Alexander, like one of the earlier Chinese monarchs, was a maniac; he wanted to wipe out the memory of earlier great emperors of early days. Kutaib did the same what was done in Java (Indonesia) later on and in India by Bakhtiyar Khilji. Overall result was the paucity of literature. Thus, most of the materials on which one had to rely was on Chinese and Tibetan records. The Chinese literally translate the terms in their language, put the ideogram for them and pronounce accordingly. Thus Kumarajiva, the most famous Buddhist scholar, becomes Thun-sheu, meaning 'boy age' or 'a longevity', in Chinese. Vimalākṣa becomes 'Wu-Keu-Yen', meaning 'without dirt-eye', and Dharmagupta (meaning 'law-secret' or 'law-repository') becomes Ta-mo-Kiu-to. The name of famous Chinese pilgrim and scholar Hiuen-tsang is variously written as Swen Chang, Jvan Jvan, Hsuan-tsang, Hiuen Tsang, Hiuen tsang, Hiuen Tsiang, Yuan Chuang, Jwan Jwan and Xuanzang. Thus there is a lot of anarchy in the nomenclature.

Prefixes denoting the nationality, such as, Ngan- for the Parthians, Che- for the Yueh-ches, Po- for the Kucheans are also added by the Chinese before names of the persons of different nationalities. The name of the Parthian Buddhist monk, Lokottama, in Chinese is Ngan-She-Kao; another Parthian monk is Ngan-hivan. Kang- was prefixed before the Sogdian names, as the ancient names of the Sogdian community was Kang.

It may be interesting to note the different names of some places, rivers, communities, etc. of the region. Khotan, the most important outpost on southern silk route, was perhaps the oldest one in Central

Asia. It was established at the time of Ashoka with the blinded prince Kuṇāl as its ruler. It figures in Sanskrit, Prakrit, Chinese, Manchu, Mongol and Tibetan records with names, such as, Sanskrit: Kustana, Kutsana and Kutsanaka; Prakrit: Khotamina, Khotamna, Khodana and Khotana; Kharosthi documents: Kustana, Khotana, Godana, Khodana, Khodamn; K'iu-sa-ta-na, like Sanskrit –Kustana; Chinese: Chien-tun, Chu-sa-tan-na, Chutan, Ho-tien, Huan-na, Huo-tan, Yo-tien, Yu-tien, Yu-tun; ancient Chinese names of the country like Khotana, Goana, –Yu-t'ien (oldest form), Yu-tun, K'iu-tan, Huo-tan, and Kiu-sa-tan-na; Manchu: Ho-thian; Mongol – Hu-t'an, O-duan, Wa-duan, Wu-duan; Tibetan – Li-yul (country), U-then, Ho-then, U-than (capital)[1] .

Cokkuka (presently Karghahalik-Yarkand) was called Tsu-ku, So-kiu, Che-kiu-kia, etc. by the Chinese, and again, Tseu-ho (in Tang Anals); Cu-g-pan in Tibetan texts; the alternative names were He-ku-po, Che-ku-pan[2]; the princes of Cokkuka were Suryabhadra, Suryasome, who went to Kashgar towards the end of fourth century A.D. to receive initiation from Kumarjiva and to study Mahayana.

Modern Balkh was called Bāhlika in Sanskrit literature, Bactria and Bactriana by the Greeks and Foho/Fo-ho by the Chinese. Ancient Bhāruka and ancient Agnideśa are known as Aksu and Turfan respectively. Bhāruka of Sanskrit documents, the modern Aksu, seems to have been derived from corrupt Sanskrit name 'Bālukā' (sand; Turkik, kum = sand). Its Chinese names are Ki-me or Ku-me.

Kuchā in Sanskrit is Kuchi; its king was called Kuchimahārāja. In Chinese, the names are Kiu-tse, Kuei-tse and Kiu-yi. The term 'Kushaṇ' is derived from Kuchi; people of Kuchi, Aksu, Kārāsahr and Turfān were of the same stock. Modern Karasahr (in old documents, A-ki-ni, derived from Sanskrit 'Agni'; king was called Agnimahārāja[3]; is mentioned in earlier Chinese sources as Yen-ki, Wu-ki, Wu-yi. Kashgar and Kashgarh is derived from Indian name Khasha or Khashya; Khashyalipi (Lalitavistara; script); Kasia ori (Ptolemy, country) and Arabic names 'Kashgar' and 'Qashqar' have also identical derivations. Chinese name is 'Hu' meaning 'barbarian'; ancient Chinese name, Shu-lei or Su-li, is based on local names Surik and Sulik; more commonly used 'Kia-sha' is supposedly based on Khasha. Tibetan 'Ga-'jag' is preserved in old Niya document as Amjaka; Tibetan name is 'Kancaki' also.[4]

Kroraina (also written as Krorāyina) of the Kharoshthi documents, transcribed in Chinese as 'Lou-lan' or 'Loulan', and Na-fo-p'o were the Chinese names of the region. The Chinese changed the name to 'Shan-Shan' in 77 B.C. The region has two cities: Charklik (Chinese: Yu-ni, 'the old town'; Tibetan: 'Great Nob') and Miran (Chinese: Hsiun, 'the new town'; Tibetan Little Nob'). Kapisha of ancient time has become Kabul.

Sarikol (place name) is modern Tashkurgan; as mentioned by Huen-tsang, the ancient dynasty of Sarikol claimed its origin from solar dynasty. Its Chinese name is Ho-pan-to. The Pamir is Tsung-ling. Tokharestan is also written as Tokharistan, Dusanbe as Diushandbe. Termez, also named Ta-mi, is also written as Termiz. The Chinese name of Gaz is Kie-chi. Sogdiana or Soghdiana, with its Centre at Samarkand, north of Tokharestan, is the 'K'ang-kiu' of Chinese Annals. The Sogdian people are also called K'ang-kiiu by the Chinese. In Sanskrit, Sogdians were called Kaṅka, also Kaṅg. The term used for them by the Indians was also Sūlikā, and also Chūlikā; in Avesta Sughda and in *Bahistun* inscriptions, the name 'Suguda' is used. Iranians called them Sughdic and Suwalic; Herodotus used the term 'Sodoi'.

It is interesting to note the names of the places of the Central Asia, and its neighbourhood, visited by the scholar pilgrims, like Fa-hien, Song-yun, Hiuen-tsang, Wu-kong and others. Some of the place names, not mentioned above, with their Chinese names in the parentheses, are: Yarkand (Kao-chang, near Turfan), Karasahr (A-ki-ni), Kucha (Kiu-che), Yak-aryk (Po-lu-kia), Yarkhoto (near Turfan; Kao-chang), Badakshan (Pa-to-ch'uang-na), Yamgan (Ying-po-kien; the valley of Koksha), Kandut (Hun-t'o-lo), Tash-kurghan (Kie-pan-t'o; Kiuan-yu-mo), Kasghar (also, Kashgar and Kashi; Kia-she, Ngan-si, Su-lei; Shu-lei), Ferghana (also Ferganah; Ta-wan), Karghalik (Che-kiu-kia; Tseu-ho), Yarkand (So-kiu), Balkh (Yue-che), Parthia (Ngan-si), Turfan (Kiue-she; the ancient capital of the kingdom of Lou-lan), Pamir (Kizil rabat, Po-mi, Chung-ling), Kunduz (Huo). Some other areas/places on the route to India were: Wakhan (Hu-mi, Pa-ho), Chitral (She-mi), the mountain region to the north of Chitral (Po-che), Bolor (Po-lu-lo; the Indus region by the valley of Yasin and Gilgit), Khottal (Ku-tu), Karategin (Kumrdh, Kiu-mi-che), Sighnan (Ch'e-ni), etc.

Scythians were called by different names by different people.

They are Śaka of the Indian literature. They were known in Persia/ Iran as Saka, Skuthoi by the Greek writers, Ashkuzai by the Assyrians, Sei (Sek) by the Chinese. China named Tsiou kokue by the Japanese, Djoua kwok by Tongkingese Alai prai dai by the Burmese, Doulimba-I Gouroun by the Manchu, Scythians of the Romans, Sacae of the Greeks, Haphtalites or White Huns of the Byzantines, Yue-tchi of the Chinese—were the same. Some other names are:

Huṇa (Sanskrit), Hun -, Hiung-nu—in Chinese

Uigur/Uighur; Toguz-Oguz/Tokuz-Oguz;

Khan, Kaha, Qaghan, etc.

China/Khitai;

Ju-jun, Avar, Khe-li, Ghei tribes;

Hephtals, Eptolits or Ephtals (by Greeks/Armenians White Huns/White Persians.

The old Sanskrit names of the rivers of the region has also changed to a large extent. Sita river of the *Purāṇas*, also written in modern books as Hsita and His-to, is present day's Yarkand darya, as also the Tarim river. Kubha is Kabul; Gomati is Gomal. Vaksu or Caksu is Oxus river and of today's Amu darya.

References

1. P.C. Bagchi, *India and Central Asia*, p.49.
2. *Ibid.*, pp. 48-49.
3. *Ibid.*, pp. 67-68.
4. *Ibid.*, pp. 43-44.

14

Perceptional Haziness in Understanding Central Asia

Indians have very few scholars who properly understand India-Central Asia relations in time-depth and proper perspective. Our scholars follow uni-track medium; most of them know only English, which is their medium of expression and writing. But for in-depth study of Central Asia, and its relations with India, the knowledge of many languages, especially, Russian, French, German, Chinese, Tibetan, Persian and Turkish, is needed. This can be done by dedicated team work. This is necessary because Russian, French and German scholars have done commendable work in the field of exploration and study of Central Asia and their works are available mostly in their respective languages; the Chinese and Tibetan languages, apart from huge material on history and culture of the region, have preserved vast treasure of the translations of the Sanskrit texts hitherto lost. Moreover, as discussed below, the original local literature about the region, was lost. But, the task of the study of Central Asia is necessary for India, because there is so much of India in Central Asia and the *vice versa.* Needless to say that, the *proper study of the region is needed for proper understanding of India's history, culture and religion, and obviously for India's self-portraiture.*

In the arena of knowledge, we had clearly two traditions. One was the tradition of collecting the knowledge from anywhere and everywhere, putting it in the wide frame of one's experience, then synthesizing and accepting it. Indians did it; they acquired knowledge the *Yogic* way; accepted it. This tradition leads one to acquire the sources of knowledge. The Chinese took the extreme steps of acquiring the sources of knowledge even by the use of force. They attacked the state of Champa in Central Vietnam for acquiring Sanskrit texts; fought war with Khotan for *Buddhist Sutras.* China wanted to have the Great

Buddhist scholar, Kumarajiva, and on denial by the king of Kuchi (*Kuchimaharaja,* the then king of present day Kuchar of Chinese Turkistan) waged war, in which Kuchi was defeated and the king was killed. Yet another Central Asian scholar was also taken to a State of China by force.

Yet the other tradition, rather than acquiring the sources of knowledge, believed in the destruction of the same and to replace them. Either blind faith in one's assumed historic role, as we find in the case of Alexander, or acceptance of the given ideology or belief system or dogma, with closed mind, as we find in the case of the Arabs and Kutaib, their General and Governor in Central Asia, leads to such situation. Central Asia witnessed the loss of its treasure of knowledge at least twice due to them. This phenomenon was repeated a number of times, the books and institutions, like Navabahar, were not only destroyed in Balkh, Bukhara and Merv, but even up to the far east in Tarim basin, and the scholars were killed.

Alexander was the first to destroy the intellectual wealth of Iran and Trans-Oxiana (Central Asia). He "allowed most of the literature of Iran to be destroyed and Greek was substituted as the official language during the four centuries of Parthian rule. These kings considered themselves philhellenes and suppressed official expression in Iranian terms. But with the outburst of Iranian nationalism fostered by the Sassanid dynasty, the Old Persian, which had always been the language of the people, reappeared in the form of Pahlavi (Pehlevi), or Middle Persian. One of the main documents is the great inscription found at Paikuli (dated about 293 A.D.). There were dialects such as the Middle Parthian in the north, Middle Sogdian in the northeast (which had a revival in the ninth century A.D.), and the Middle Sacian in the east." (*Encyclopedia Americana,* Vol. 15; 1965 edition; p. 306).

The next was the Arabian General Qutaiba ibn Muslim, who conquered Khorezm, Soghd, Tukharistan and Ferghana in the beginning of the eighth century A.D. Not only the old writings of the Central Asian people were destroyed, making the investigation and research on various aspects of the society and culture of the people extremely difficult, but even the scholars were killed. Eminent Central Asian scholar Abu'l-Rayhan al-Biruni writes about the same: "And Qutaiba killed the people that knew well Khorezmian writings and knew their legends and taught (the sciences) that existed among the Khorezmians: he inflicted on them many torments and (these legends) became so secret that it was impossible to learn for sure what had happened even to the Khorezmians after the rise of Islam" [Quoted by M. Asimov in his paper, *Science in Central Asia and the Method of Studying it*, in "Kushan Studies in U.S.S.R., Calcutta (1970), p.18)].

India, Central Asia and Iran formed part of a composite religious, cultural, linguistic continuum since remotest past. Ethnic, political, economic and trade links between them also used to be equally intimate and deep. The suppression of the Iranian language, which started from the very beginning of the Arab rule, had negative impact on intellectual climate of the region. It needs mention that either Iranian or its dialects — which were also the dialects of Sanskrit — as Niya or Gandhari Prakrit in the Tarim basin and Chulika Paisachi Prakrit in Sogdiana — were spoken in Southern Central Asia. As is well-known, "The Arab conquest of 641 A.D. imposed Arabic upon Iran, except where heretical groups persisted in the preservation of the old literature in secret. A colony of Persians who refused to accept Islam migrated to India, taking their religious books with them, and thus preserved a mass of literature which probably would have been lost in Iran. These Parsis still utilize the Avestic or Pahlavi for their ritualistic devotions." (*Ibid.*) During the Samanid period (a native Persian dynasty; 874-999 A.D.), however, the great counter reaction to Arabic brought renaissance of Persian. In the aftermath of the same great literary pieces, such as Firdausi's *Shah Nameh* were written (Encyclopedia, *op. cit.*). It was this kind of the fear of the destruction of the intellectual treasure that thousands of books were hidden in Tunhuang.

As we know, thousands of texts, mostly of Sanskrit and Prakrit in Brahmi and Kharosthi scripts, were discovered during last two centuries in Central Asia. 20,000 manuscripts of different languages in Brahmi, Kharosthi, Persian, Tibetan, Turki, Uighur and Tokharian scripts, walled up for 900 years for protection against invaders, were found from Tun-huang alone (B.N. Puri; *Buddhism in Central Asia*; pp. 23-24; Eliot, *Hinduism and Buddhism* III, p. 189).

At least one more such example of hiding the texts due to fear of destruction, a phenomenon parallel to Tunhuang, may be cited here. In December 1945, a jar, containing Coptic translations made more than 1,600 years ago of the texts of 120-150 A.D., and even of

50-100 A.D., written in Greek, was discovered on the cliff of the Jabal al-Tarif, near Nag Hammadi, in Upper Egypt, by a peasant, Muhammad Ali. His mother, thinking it useless, burnt some of the papyrus to make a fire in the evening, but enough still remained. These remaining manuscript finds of Egypt were the texts of the 55 Gnostic Gospels; Elaine Pagels, Weidenfeld and Nicolson based their *Gnostic Gospels* on these hidden manuscript finds.

As we know, Christianity was Judaic in origin. In its efforts to enter the Gentile, it had to seek a new idiom; made an alliance with the *Gnosticism,* the then religion of the Greco-Roman elite in one form or the other. But the Christianity and Gnosticism differed in their basics. Unlike Christianity, the soul of Gnosticism was spiritual and philosophical, rather than apocalyptical, millennial, historical and literalist; it did not believe in the otherness of God. Unlike Orthodox Christianity, which was organizational, the Gnostic Christianity was subversive of any authority. Obviously, the alliance was a mismatch and tolerated till orthodox Christianity became powerful. Ultimately, when Emperor Constantine became Christian, Christianity became State religion, the Gnostic books were banned and destroyed. In 367 A.D., Athanasius, the powerful Archbishop of Alexandria, sent out orders for purging all apocryphal books with heretical tendency. Serapeum, in Alexandria in Egypt, which preserved treasures of ancient learning and housed the famous Alexandria library, was reduced to ashes when destroyed by Theophilus, a saint, and a friend of St. Xerome. Naturally, under such circumstances, some Gnostic Christian monks hid the texts to save them, what the others did later on in Tunhuang, thousands of kilometres away. All such developments resulted in India and Central Asia spending centuries in forgetfulness of the self as well as each other. And it is only now the two regions are discovering their self, as well as their mutual relations.

Apart from the loss of literature, the colonial myths, such as 'Aryan Aggression Theory' (now Aryan Migration Theory); over-emphasis on race, migration and conflict between nomads and sedentary people; Euro and Middle-East-centrism and other biases of the Western scholars, disorganized facts, anarchy even in nomenclature of place and personal names, etc. come in the way of our proper understanding of the subject, and thus create perceptional haziness. It is not possible to cover these topics in a short write-up. It needs elaboration and detailed study.

Nomadism in Central Asia, as elsewhere, was a way of life dictated by nature and geography. It is not correct to term the nomads 'savage and barbaric', as they had developed metallurgy. It is also not correct to say that nomads and sedentary people of the region always fought wars with each other. After all, Alexander found towns and even villages unprotected and without protective walls. One of the reasons of massive migration was the climate change due to prolonged desiccation. Some people migrated; a section was absorbed in the in-coming hordes.

The discovery of Sanskrit gave new identity and historical time-depth to Europe. Euro-American scholars were enchanted; searched their roots in India. The first category of scholars, as they were, emerging after India's encounter with the West, was mainly concerned with seeking the knowledge. But a second category also emerged, whose only concern was the promotion of the colonial Euro-Christian interest; they wanted colonization to grow and get strengthened; they also wanted to win India for Christ. This was the reason that they indulged in myth-making. As Central Asia was also colonized, the region must have some impact of the same, as we have in India. Taking history in time-depth and freeing the historical and cultural discourse from colonial myths and at new intellectual height shall help us in getting rid of much confusion.

In India, our history and literature does not support westward migration. The direction of phonetic changes between two intimately linked languages — Vedic Sanskrit and Old Irani — is from the former to the latter. This sets the direction of migration from east to west.

A particular difficulty, which every student of Central Asia faces, crops up due to multiplicity in the names of the Places, persons, etc. The situation here is almost anarchical. As for example, Khotan, the most important outpost on southern silk route, and perhaps the oldest one in Central Asia, established at the time of Ashoka with the blinded prince Kunal as its ruler in about 240 B.C., has as many names as given hereafter: It figures in Sanskrit, Prakrit, Chinese, Manchu, Mongol and Tibetan records with names, such as, Sanskrit — Kutsana and Kutsanaka; Prakrit — Khotamina, Khotamna, Khodana and Khotana; Chinese — Chien-tun, Chu-sa-tan-na, Chutan, Ho-tien, Huan-na, Huo-tan, Yo-tien, Yu-tien, Yu-tun; Manchu — Ho-thian; Mongol — Hu-t'an, O-duan, Wa-duan,

Wu-duan; Tibetan — Li-yul, U-then, Ho-then. Even the name of famous Chinese pilgrim and scholar Hiuen-tsang is variously written as Swen Chang, Jvan Jvan, Hsuan-tsang, Hiuen Tsang, Hiuen tsang, Hiuen Tsiang, Yuan Chuang, Jwan Jwan and Xuanzang. This clearly shows that there is a lot of anarchy in the nomenclature. However, in spite of the perceptional haziness, which comes in the way of a scholar in understanding Central Asia, the endeavour becomes highly rewarding.

ANNEXURE

Kumarjiva and his Works

Kumarajiva's story is a reminder that the nation hasn't shrunk territorially in 1947 alone; the process has been going on since the past two millennia at least.

India shrinking

The story of Kumarajiva is important to understand two things we Indians, pretentiously aping to be 'liberals", prefer to ignore. One, India hasn't shrunk terrirorially in 1947 alone; the process has been going on uninterruptedly since the past two millennia at least. Two, historically, India never had problems with Buddhist/Confucius China. It had — and continues to have— problems with Communist China; remove this perverse ideology, and India and China are *bhai-bhai.* Herein lies the importance of Nirmala Sharma's *Kumarajiva : The Transcreator of Buddhist Chinese Diction,* which not only talks about the Buddhist Scholar's religious activities, but also highlights his translation—or transcreation — works.

Kumarajiva's life shows that 2,000 years ago, the cultural India wasn't confined to the Himalayas. In fact, it flourished to the north of the Himalayas as it prospered within India.

So, who was Kumarajiva? Son of Kashmiri father Kumarayana and Kuchean mother Jiva, Kumarajiva was a great transcreator of the Buddhist Chinese diction. He developed a new translation methodology. Of course, the translation of Sanskrit texts into Chinese was a joint enterprise. Among the translators of Buddhist Sanskrit literature in Chinese, six or seven were Chinese, six Indians, and 16 Central Asians.

Book Review : *Kumarajiva : The Transcreator* of Buddhist-Chinese Diction; Nirmala Sharma, Niyogi, New Delhi, 2011, Rs. 2,000. Published in the *Pioneer*, New Delhi.

Kucha, from where Kumarajiva's mother came, in northern Tarim basin, exists in the present-day Xinjiang/Chinese Turkistan and was a centre of Buddhist learning. Such was the importance of Kucha that it was from here that Indian music had spread to China. The place also excelled in painting and dance. Hundreds of Sanskrit manuscripts, murals and scrolls have been discovered from Kucha and elsewhere in Tarim valley. Here, it needs to be mentioned that Yarkand and Khotan in northern Tarim valley were centres of Mahayana Buddhism, while Kashgar, Kucha, Turfan and Shan Shan near Lobnor were centres of Hinayana Buddhism.

Central Asia, like India, had great centres of learning. No wonder, Kumarajiva, after learning Buddhist scriptures in Kashmir, studied four *Vedas,* five sciences, Brahmanical *Shastràs* and Astronomy in Kashgar. This shows that the scholarly environment was not of Hindu-Buddhist dichotomy, but of continuum, as the scholarship was not confined to the study of the Buddhist scriptures.

Kumarajiva, like scores of other Central Asian scholars, contributed immensely towards the dissemination of Buddhist religion and thought in Central Asia and China. However, the tradition of translation of Sanskrit texts in China was well-established before he arrived here. A Parthian crown prince. An Shih-kao (Chinese name), had abdicated his throne in favour of his uncle, and dedicated his life to Buddhism. He went to the East (China) and settled in Loyang in 148 A.D. He ended up translating up to 170 Sanskrit texts in Chinese.

Kumarajiva was a great scholar. The "nations of the west" (India and Central Asia), in Chinese parlance, acknowledged his genius. Soon, his fame spread towards the east, provoking Chinese king Fu Chien to first dispatch an envoy and then an army to bring Kumarjiva to China.

Kumarajiva advised the king of Kucha not to fight the Chinese, but the king ignored his advice, and was killed in the battlefield. Kumarajiva was taken to China as a captive, but was honoured by the emperor.

In China, Kumarajiva translated a large number of texts into Sanskrit; many of them have been lost and only their references are available today. However, he is particularly famous for the translation of *Lotus Sutra.* completed in 406 A.D. and *The Treatise on the Great Prajnaparamita.*

Kumarajiva improved the technique to translation prevailing in China. The procedure was simple but rigorous : First Kumarajiva used to explain the meaning of the text twice; the monks then discussed the same among themselves and translated it in literary Chinese. Thereafter, Kumarajiva would repeatedly compare the translation with the original Sanskrit text, thus arriving at definite version both in terms of thought and Chinese aesthetics. Being concerned with the essence of the text; he avoided word-to-word translation; he shortened the text by deleting repetitions and ponderous verbosity intolerable to Chinese literati, making the final version more appealing to Chinese literary tastes. Kumarajiva, it is said, had more than 3,000 monk disciples, including Tao-sheng, Sheng-chao, Tao-jung and Seng-jui. Shramana Seng-jui, the biographer and constant companion of Kumarajiva, possessed extraordinary talent and wisdom. Whenever the two disputed about the rhythmic structure of the Indian language, and its common features and differences, Jui would say : "The national custom of India emphasises the literary form and considers those forms good whose music and rhythm suit that of stringed instruments." In this case, a remark about the Chinese translation is worth mentioning "When one translates the Indian language into Chinese, it loses its elegance. Even though the general meaning is reproduced the style is to a large extent lost. It is as if one (first) chews the rice before giving it to another; not only does it deny him the taste, it also makes him spit it out."

This reviewer shares the view expressed in the book that "Kumarajiva's charismatic diction has cast its sheen on the succeeding centuries in East Asian lands." His style has been the radiance of Buddhism. And it was his translation of *Satya-Siddhi Shastra* that gave rise to Hsieh-ho's *Six Principles of Chinese Painting,* which still remains the basis of theoretical discussions on the aesthetics of poetry, painting, sculpture and calligraphy in East Asia.

The book must be read by one and all.

Index